P9-BTO-749

"In an age where too many 'Bible' studies fail to open the Bible—or, if opened, fail to touch on the actual themes in the text itself—Nancy Guthrie immerses us in the wisdom of the Word. How refreshing! With her keen observations, penetrating applications, and thoughtful, engaging questions, Nancy Guthrie's latest study on the Old Testament Wisdom Books and the Psalms gets us to see and smell, taste and touch, and understand and apply the everyday wisdom of Christ—our creator and crucified Lord."

Douglas O'Donnell, Senior Pastor, New Covenant Church, Naperville, Illinois; author, *The Beginning and End of Wisdom*

"I love Nancy's infectious passion for teaching the Old Testament in a relevant, practical, spiritual, and Christ-centered way. I'm confident that this book will ignite that same passion in many others—transforming lives, families, churches, and communities."

David P. Murray, Professor of Old Testament and Practical Theology, Puritan Reformed Theological Seminary

"In this study guide, Nancy Guthrie shows how the Old Testament Wisdom Books and the Psalms provide practical life lessons for Christians and stand as pointers to the supreme wisdom of God in the life, death, and resurrection of Jesus. With great skill she leads the reader to the heart of each book being studied and demonstrates its place in Scripture as a testimony to Christ. Christian readers are encouraged to read the Old Testament Wisdom Literature in light of the relationship we have with Christ, who is the power and wisdom of God."

Graeme Goldsworthy, Visiting Lecturer in Hermeneutics, Moore Theological College

~Praise for the Series~

"The Bible is a book about Jesus. The disciples walking to Emmaus after the resurrection discovered this as Christ himself walked along with them and explained how the Old Testament pointed to the Savior. This important series by Nancy Guthrie spotlights how Jesus can be seen throughout the Old Testament. I recommend the entire series to you."

Alistair Begg, Senior Pastor, Parkside Church, Chagrin Falls, Ohio

"It's not hyperbole to say, 'It's about time.' While there are good books out there telling pastors how to preach Christ from all the Scriptures, there have been very few Bible studies for laypeople—especially for women—along these lines. Nancy Guthrie does an amazing job of helping us to fit the pieces of the biblical puzzle together, with Christ at the center."

Michael S. Horton, J. Gresham Machen Professor of Systematic Theology and Apologetics, Westminster Seminary California

"Nancy takes us by the hand and the heart on an exegetical excursion to see Christ in the Old Testament. The beauty of Guthrie's writing is that you are certain she has met him there first."

Jean F. Larroux, Senior Pastor, Southwood Presbyterian Church, PCA, Huntsville, Alabama

"There are many great Christian books, but not many great Bible studies. Nancy is a master of getting the Word of God into the mouths, hearts, and lives of her students. I cannot wait to share these studies with my people."

Donna Dobbs, Christian Education Director, First Presbyterian Church, Jackson, Mississippi

The Wisdom
of God

Other books in the Seeing Jesus in the Old Testament series:

The Promised One

The Lamb of God

The Wisdom of God

Seeing Jesus in the Psalms
& Wisdom Books

(A 10-Week Bible Study)

nancy guthrie

WHEATON, ILLINOIS

The Wisdom of God: Seeing Jesus in the Psalms and Wisdom Books

Copyright © 2012 by Nancy Guthrie

Published by Crossway
        1300 Crescent Street
        Wheaton, Illinois 60187

All rights reserved. No part of this publication may be reproduced, stored in a retrieval system, or transmitted in any form by any means, electronic, mechanical, photocopy, recording, or otherwise, without the prior permission of the publisher, except as provided for by USA copyright law.

Cover design: Amy Bristow

Cover image: The Golden Violin, c.1898 (oil on canvas)
        by Maxwell Ashby Armfield (1882–1972)
        Private Collection / The Bridgeman Art Library

First printing 2012

Printed in the United States of America

Unless otherwise indicated, scripture quotations are from the ESV® Bible (*The Holy Bible, English Standard Version*®), copyright © 2001 by Crossway. Used by permission. All rights reserved.

Scripture quotations marked MESSAGE are from *The Message*. Copyright © by Eugene H. Peterson 1993, 1994, 1995, 1996, 2000, 2001, 2002. Used by permission of NavPress Publishing Group.

Scripture references marked NIV are taken from The Holy Bible, New International Version®, NIV. Copyright © 1973, 1978, 1984 by Biblica, Inc.™ Used by permission. All rights reserved worldwide.

Scripture references marked NLT are from *The Holy Bible, New Living Translation*, copyright © 1996, 2004. Used by permission of Tyndale House Publishers, Inc., Wheaton, Ill., 60189. All rights reserved.

All emphases in Scripture quotations have been added by the author.

Trade paperback ISBN: 978-1-4335-2632-9
PDF ISBN: 978-1-4335-2633-6
Mobipocket ISBN: 978-1-4335-2634-3
ePub ISBN: 978-1-4335-2635-0

Library of Congress Cataloging-in-Publication Data
Guthrie, Nancy.
  The wisdom of God : seeing Jesus in the Psalms and wisdom books / Nancy Guthrie.
    p. cm. (Seeing Jesus in the Old Testament)
    ISBN 978-1-4335-2632-9 (tp)
    1. Bible O.T. Psalms—Textbooks. 2. Bible. O.T. Psalms—Criticism, interpretation, etc. 3. Wisdom literature—Textbooks. 4. Wisdom literature—Criticism, interpretation, etc. 5. Jesus Christ—Biblical teaching. I. Title.
BS1456.G88   2012
223'.0607—dc23   2011025567

Crossway is a publishing ministry of Good News Publishers.

VP		24	23	22	21	20	19	18	17	16	15	14
16	15	14	13	12	11	10	9	8	7	6	5	4	3

To my wise husband of twenty-five years and counting,
David Guthrie.

My beloved is mine, and I am his.
—*Song of Solomon 2:16*

Contents

Before We Get Started

A Note from Nancy

I like to think of myself as smart; I know stuff. In fact, it seems as good a time as any to make it known that I was robbed of being my high school class valedictorian by the A- I got in driver's education during the summer before my sophomore year. But I'm not bitter. (Okay, maybe a little.) Of course there are some things I find it convenient not to know—like how to work my husband's espresso machine. And there are some things I try to understand that make me feel like I have rocks for brains—like how the stock market works or what the mechanic tried to explain to me about the problem with my car.

But there is something I want far more than to be smart. And that is to be wise. And I don't want to settle for what the world labels as wisdom. I want to have the wisdom that comes only from being given the gift of wisdom that God generously gives to his own. He has given us the entire Old and New Testaments that we might grow in wisdom and knowledge. But I'm also not talking about just knowing more about the Bible. Because we can have all the right Sunday school answers and still not be truly wise.

What I want, and what I believe you must want if you have opened up this book to do this study, is to have the wisdom of God that is ours only through a relationship with the incarnation of the wisdom of God, Jesus Christ. And the way we come to know him in a more intimate and transforming way is to listen to him speak to us and to chew on what he has to say, allowing it to work its way through our thinking and our emotions and our will so that it comes out in our day-to-day lives as wisdom.

So welcome to *The Wisdom of God: Seeing Jesus in the Psalms and Wisdom Books.* I'm so glad you have committed to set time aside to look into God's Word along with me through this book. Paul wrote to Timothy, "From childhood you have been acquainted with the sacred writings, which are able to make you wise for salvation through faith in Christ Jesus" (2 Tim. 3:15). He was saying that the Old Testament was able to make Timothy wise so that he could see and embrace Jesus Christ. And as we open up Job, Psalms, Proverbs, Ecclesiastes, and Song of Solomon, that is what we want—to be made "wise for salvation through faith in Christ Jesus." Again and again Jesus himself made it clear that we can search the Old Testament Scriptures and find him there. This study is uniquely designed to help you to look into the wonder of the wisdom literature of the Old Testament and see how it prepares us for and points us toward Christ.

There are three essential parts to this study. The first is the personal time you will spend reading your Bible, seeking to strengthen your grip on its truths as you work your way through the questions provided in the Personal Bible Study section of each week's lesson. This will be the easiest part to skip. But nothing is more important than reading and studying God's Word expecting that he will meet you as you do.

As you work on the Personal Bible Study, don't become frustrated if you can't come up with an answer to every question or if you're not sure what the question is getting at. I am hoping that the questions will get you into the passage and get you thinking it through in a fresh way. The goal is not necessarily to record all of the "right" answers but to interact with the passage and grow in your understanding. Certainly some answers to your lingering questions will become clearer as you read the Teaching Chapter and as you discuss the passage with your group.

The second part of each lesson is the Teaching Chapter, in which I seek to explain and apply the passage we are studying. At the end of each Teaching Chapter is a short piece called "Looking Forward" that will turn your attention to how what we've just studied in that part of the wisdom literature gives us insight into what is still to come when Christ returns. The wisdom of God helps us understand not just the history of what God has done to glorify himself through redemption but what he is doing now and what is still to come when his wise plan comes to its glorious conclusion, or we might say, its "glorious new beginning," in the new heaven and the new earth.

The third part of each week's lesson is the time you spend with your group sharing your lives together and discussing what you've learned and what you're still trying to understand and apply. A discussion guide is included at the end of each week's lesson. You may want to follow it exactly, working through each question as written. Or you may just want to use the guide as an idea starter for your discussion.

Each aspect is important—laying the foundation, building on it, and sealing it in. We all have different learning styles, so one aspect of the study will likely have more impact on you than another, but all three together will help you to truly "own" the truths in this study so that they can become a part of you as you seek to know your covenant God in deeper ways.

I've put the sections of this study together in a way that offers flexibility for how you can use it and flexibility in how you can schedule your time working through it. If you are going to use it for a ten-week group study, you will want to read the Teaching Chapter in Week 1, "The Wisdom Hidden in the Wisdom Books," before the first meeting. (There is no Personal Bible Study section for the first week.) From then on, each week participants will want to come to the group time having completed the Personal Bible Study section of the next week's lesson as well as having read the Teaching Chapter. You may want to put a star beside questions in the Personal Bible Study and underline key passages in the chapter that you want to be sure to bring up in the discussion. During your time together each week you will use the Discussion Guide to talk through the big ideas of the week's lesson.

There is a great deal of material here, and you may want to take your time with it, giving more time to discuss its foundational truths, allowing it to sink in. To expand the study over twenty weeks, you would break each Week into two parts, spending one week on the Personal Bible Study section—either doing it on your own and discussing your answers when you meet, or actually working through the questions together when you meet. Then, you would ask group members to read the chapter on their own over the next week and use the discussion guide to discuss the big ideas of the lesson the following week.

If you are leading a group study, we would like to provide you with some resources that have been developed specifically for this study. We hope that these resources will increase your confidence in leading the group. To request those helps, go to http://www.SeeingJesusintheOldTestament.com.

I am praying that as you see the Wisdom of God—Jesus himself—in a fresh way through this study over the coming weeks, he will "make you wise for salvation" and that you will walk through this life and one day into his presence as one who is truly wise.

—*Nancy Guthrie*

Week 1

The Wisdom Hidden in the Wisdom Books

Teaching Chapter

What We Need Most to Know

When someone speaking to me begins a sentence with "God told me," I have to admit that it sends up a red flag for me, especially if it is not followed by a verse of Scripture. Perhaps I should think that the person saying it is so incredibly spiritual and sensitive that he has an ongoing conversation with God in which God speaks to him clearly and directly, giving him specific extrabiblical instructions about what to do and where to go. Certainly, many people today see this as the way we should expect to receive guidance from God if we are in intimate relationship with him.

A while ago, a friend of mine gave me a copy of a new book by an author who has had multiple books on the best-seller list, and because I've read other books by this author that I found tremendously insightful, I looked forward to reading it. The book's premise is that a conversational relationship with God is not only available but meant to be normative, and that if you are not hearing God speak to you in this way, something is wrong with your spiritual life. The author encouraged his readers to still themselves in a posture of surrender and begin by asking the Lord questions about small matters that are not addressed in Scripture, offering examples from his own experience throughout the book: asking God if he should paint the bathroom, where he could find his missing watch, and what dogs do after they die.

Certainly having a relationship with God in which you hear him answer your questions and tell you clearly what to do in every aspect of life is very appealing. We all want wisdom for making decisions that will be pleasing to God.

As I continued to read the book, I came to an account of a horse-riding accident. The author writes that he thinks he remembered to ask God about riding the horse but realizes he did not ask *where* he should ride.

What do you think? Is this really the *normative* way for the Christian to go about life in this world—listening for a word from God about every choice and decision we have in front of us? Should I pray about which socks to wear today or what to make for dinner tonight and wait to move forward until I hear him speak to me inside my head?

At the risk that you will deem me thoroughly unspiritual and disconnected from God and put this book down before we barely get started, I have to tell you that I have never heard God speak to me in this way.[1] This is not to say that God never speaks to believers today in this way.[2] And it is not to say that I haven't heard the voice of God clearly in my life. I could talk with you for hours about specific ways God has spoken to me as I have read, studied, and heard his Word preached and taught. He has spoken to me clear words of conviction, instruction, warning, encouragement, assurance, comfort, promise, and guidance regarding his will for my life in powerful ways so that I knew he was speaking directly to my heart and my circumstances. But I would never claim to say authoritatively that God told me something that I cannot find in the Bible.

While the super-spiritual may expect to hear a direct word from God internally or externally through their circumstances so that they will know what to do and what is right, on the opposite spectrum, most of our culture assumes that God has nothing relevant to say to them about how they live and the choices they make. While they might consult the latest self-help book on the best-seller list, or tune in to the latest self-help guru, or look around at the larger culture to absorb its values and moral sense of right and wrong, seeking out God's perspective on the matter would never occur to them. Most people in this world live their lives and make their decisions with little or no thought of God.

So how about you? Some decisions are quite easy to make—especially concerning those matters on which God has clearly spoken. Certainly we don't have to pray about whether to sleep with someone we are not married to. We have clear instructions on that. We don't have to expect to hear a word from God about whether we should forgive some-one who has hurt us. We know clearly what we should do; we just don't want to do it. What we struggle with are the things that are not directly addressed in Scripture. *Is this the person I should marry? Is this the job I should take? Should I watch this television program? Which way should I vote in this election?*

These are the things for which we need wisdom. So how do we get that wisdom? Should we expect to hear a direct word from God on these matters? And, if so, how do we know it is his voice we are hearing? Are we to make those decisions on the basis of a vague and subjective feel-ing about the Lord's will in the matter? Are we to try on one option to see if we "have a peace about it"?

Or can we make decisions in these matters freely and consciously on the basis of what the Scriptures say and the principles they contain? Is it possible that God has given us a source of wisdom that is grounded in who he is and his purposes in the world that will give us the guidance we need to make wise decisions in all matters of life in this world?

Paul writes that there is "a secret and hidden wisdom of God, which God decreed before the ages for our glory" (1 Cor. 2:7). So perhaps in our efforts to find answers to these questions, we need to start at the begin-ning, or maybe even before the beginning, when, in perfect wisdom, God's plans for his creation took shape.

The Secret Wisdom Hidden

God's revelation of himself and of his plans for this world is progres-sive. He began revealing his character and his plan in the creation of the world when he made humanity in his own image and put them in charge of the world he created. Adam and Eve's wisdom for navigating life in the perfect environment of Eden came from what God had told them and what they discovered through their own senses, interpreted in light of what God had told them. The big question was whether they would accept and obey God's clearly revealed wisdom by not eating from the tree of the knowledge of good and evil. Then the Serpent came along and implanted in Eve's mind the suggestion that God was with-holding something from them. She looked at God's prohibition and thought, "The tree was to be desired to make one wise" (Gen. 3:6). This was the first time a human being disobeyed God, thinking she knew better than God, but it certainly wasn't the last.

In fact, as a result of Adam and Eve's sin, and the curse that came upon all of creation because of it, all of us are born with a resistance to the wisdom that comes from God. But God, in his grace, has not been content to leave us living in darkness and alienation. God, over history, has continued to reveal himself. God called a people to himself and spoke to them through dreams, visions, and the prophetic word and gave them his covenant and his law. God gave his people story and symbols and shadows to prepare them to understand his wise plan, but it was not yet explicitly clear. Faith for God's people in the Old Testament era meant placing their hopes in God's promises, promises that had an element of mystery to them as to when and how they would come about (1 Pet. 1:10–12). And to guide them in living by faith as they waited for God to bring about more of his plan, God gave his people the Wisdom Literature we find in the Old Testament.

Each of the five books we'll study together deals with how to live in wisdom. They provide guidance for how to live in this world as one who belongs to God. Job shows how a wise person lives in a world in which the seemingly innocent suffer. Psalms provides the wise person with praise and prayers and laments for expressing his heart and mind to his God. Proverbs offers practical daily advice for living as a wise person in matters of relationship and work in the real world. Ecclesiastes reveals that living wisely requires not just living under the sun but under the rule of God and in the fear of God. And Song of Solomon sings a song of wisdom in regard to sexual desire and delight.

On one hand the Wisdom Books help us "to make sense of our world, and on the other hand [they] strengthen our trust in God in the face of things we cannot make sense of."[3] They address the tensions of living in a world marked by sin as we anticipate full redemption.

But as good and true as this revelation of wisdom from God was, more was needed. Just as the law served not only to provide instruction but also to reveal people's utter inability to live up to the law, so did Old Testament Wisdom Literature provide needed guidance for living while also revealing the people's inability to live in perfect wisdom. Just as the law revealed the need for One who would follow the law perfectly in their place, so the Wisdom Literature exposed the need for One who would live in perfect wisdom in their place.

The wisest person of their day was King Solomon, who ruled Israel in great wisdom, but in many ways he turned against God's wisdom and pursued his own passions. Clearly someone wiser than Solomon was needed.

The Secret Wisdom Disclosed

After centuries of waiting, the day finally came when God sent exactly what was needed. Jesus stood in the midst of the wisdom teachers of his day—the scribes and Pharisees—and told them, "Something greater than Solomon is here" (Matt. 12:42; Luke 11:31). Indeed, standing there among them was wisdom incarnate.

In Jesus we were given the wisdom of God both mediated to us as a gift and lived out before us in perfection. They called Jesus "Teacher," and in truth, he was a great wisdom teacher. Throughout the Gospel narratives Jesus is portrayed as the wise man who, in the form and content of his sayings, followed the traditions of Israel's wisdom teachers.[3] The people who heard him teach recognized that he was endowed with insight and authority that none of their other teachers had. Matthew writes that "coming to his hometown he taught them in their synagogue, so that they were astonished, and said, 'Where did this man get this wisdom and these mighty works?'" (Matt. 13:54).

> *In Jesus we were given the wisdom of God both mediated to us as a gift and lived out before us in perfection.*

Jesus's most characteristic form of teaching was the parable. Matthew explains in his Gospel that "this was to fulfill what was spoken by the prophet: 'I will open my mouth in parables; I will utter what has been hidden since the foundation of the world'" (Matt. 13:35). What was it Jesus uttered that had been hidden since the foundation of the world? It was what he said about himself, still in a somewhat hidden way through parables. The treasure hidden in a field that is worth selling everything to own? It's Jesus (Matt. 13:44). The vineyard owner's son who is killed by the evil tenants? That's Jesus (Matt. 20:33–41). The rock upon which a house and a life can be built so that it can withstand the storms that inevitably come? Jesus is that rock (Matt. 7:24). What was the "secret and hidden wisdom of God, which God decreed before the ages for our glory" (1 Cor. 2:7)? It is Jesus.

But the supreme revelation and demonstration of God's hidden wisdom was much more than Jesus's teaching on the hillside or in the synagogue. Most profoundly, it was Jesus hanging on a cross.

God's secret wisdom that was hidden is his plan to accomplish the salvation of sinners and the restoration of the perfect environment and perfect relationship he intends to share with them. That could not be accomplished merely through Jesus's living life before us so that we could learn from him and follow his example. This restored relationship could come only through his death in our place and his resurrection as the firstfruits of all who believe (1 Cor. 15:20). God's secret plan was not just sending Jesus and setting him up as the wisest of all teachers but in offering him up as a sacrifice for sin and raising him up victorious over death.

In your search for wisdom that is practical and pivotal, God wants to lead you to the foot of Christ's cross. Perhaps that makes no sense to you. Perhaps you cannot see how a man hanging on a cross in the ancient world has anything to do with your needs and concerns today in our modern world. Most people saw the cross of Christ that way in his day too. Paul wrote: "For Jews demand signs and Greeks seek wisdom, but we preach Christ crucified, a stumbling block to Jews and folly to Gentiles" (1 Cor. 1:22–23).

To see its vast wisdom, the cross must be seen in context of God's grand plan for all things, determined before the world was made, accomplished in human history, and coming to its culmination in eternity future. Perhaps you think your life is all about you and your needs and your thoughts and your questions in the here and now. My friend, you are part of a much grander story than just your little life. And the more you see your life in the context of this much bigger story, this much grander plan, the wiser you become as you live it.

The Jews of Jesus's day expected the long-awaited Messiah to come in glory and begin his reign with uncontested power, not to die like a common criminal. Similarly, the Greeks of Jesus's day who exalted reason and public philosophy considered a crucified messiah as dangerous stupidity. Yet it was God's intention that what seemed to them to be utter foolishness would put his unfathomable wisdom on display most profoundly.[4]

The devastating turn of events that put Christ on the cross was not God's plan gone terribly wrong but the fulfillment of it (see Acts 2:23–24). Paul wrote in 1 Corinthians 1:23–24 that Christ crucified is "the power of God and the wisdom of God." In fact, Paul, a very educated man, told the Corinthians that he "decided to know nothing among you except Jesus Christ and him crucified" (1 Cor. 2:2). Paul was not saying that he intended to devote himself to blissful ignorance about anything other than the cross. He was saying that everything he did and everything he thought and taught became centered on this ultimate wisdom: the cross of Christ.

Can you imagine what it would mean for you, like Paul, to put Christ crucified at the center of your life so that everything else revolves around it and emanates from it? How would it impact your Facebook status, your credit card bill, your vacation plans, your marriage or singleness, your parenting, your professional pursuits, your political involvement? Does not embracing this wisdom impact and inform every aspect of our ordinary lives?

Surely this is how the hidden wisdom of God takes root in our lives and provides us the guidance we long for—it becomes the functional center of our lives. The gospel is not simply a story; it is a power, so that when the gospel is loved and applied and enjoyed, this power goes to work on the interior of our lives, making us wise.

The Image We Are to Be Conformed To

Do you want to know God's will for your life? It is not a secret God expects you to figure out on your own or wait to hear whispered in your ear. The Bible clearly reveals God's will for us. It is that we are "to be conformed to the image of his Son" (Rom. 8:29). God wants you to walk and talk and think and live like Jesus.

One way to see how Jesus walked and talked and lived is to read the Gospels. Yet long before Jesus walked this earth, God provided his people with foreshadows of Jesus throughout the Old Testament. Over the coming weeks, as we make our way through the Wisdom Literature of the Old Testament, we'll not only find *wise principles* for living life in this world as one who belongs to God, but we'll also see the *wise person* these books point to, the wisest person who ever lived, hidden in its drama and poetry and proverb and song.

> *The gospel is not simply a story; it is a power, so that when the gospel is loved and applied and enjoyed, this power goes to work on the interior of our lives, making us wise.*

We'll begin in Job, reading a story in which a seemingly innocent man who fears God suffers in unthinkable ways and is restored, defeating Satan's destructive purposes in the process. In Job's story we'll see shadows of the greater Job, Jesus, the only perfectly innocent person who ever lived, whose life was not spared in his suffering but is now resurrected and glorified, having soundly defeated Satan's schemes.

We'll make our way through Psalms over five weeks, singing our way through the songs Jesus sang along with his fellow Israelites—the praises he sang out from his heart, the laments he cried out in his suffering, the prayers through which he expressed trust in his Father. Because these are the songs he sang, we will discover what it means to sing them *with* Christ, but we will also discover that we sing the psalms *about* Christ. He is the blessed man who does not walk in the counsel of the wicked, but his delight is in the law of the LORD (Psalm 1). He is the king set on Zion, the Son in whom we take refuge (Psalm 2). He is our good shepherd who prepares a table before us in the presence of our enemies (Psalm 23). He is the one who has clean hands and a pure heart who can ascend the hill of the LORD (Psalm 24). It is he who was truly forsaken by God (Psalm 22). It is his blood that blots out our transgressions and washes us from our iniquity (Psalm 51). It is his body that did not rot in the grave (Psalm 16). We'll also discover that we sing the psalms *to* Christ, the Lord. He is the Lord who sits enthroned forever (Ps. 9:7); he is our rock and our redeemer (Ps. 19:14); it is his beauty we want to gaze upon, his face we seek (Ps. 27:4, 8).

When we read in Proverbs that the fear of the Lord is the beginning of knowledge, and that fools despise wisdom and instruction, we'll see that Jesus is the one who truly fears the Lord, and that to fear the Lord is to believe the gospel. When the writer of Proverbs sets before us two ways—one that leads to life and one that leads to death—we'll realize that he is ultimately pointing us to Christ who is "the way, and the truth, and the life" (John 14:6).

In Ecclesiastes we'll discover that life's true meaning and purpose, which eluded the preacher, is found not in chasing after the wind but in following after Christ.

And in the love poetry of Song of Solomon we'll hear echoes of the longing we have for the lover of our souls, our beloved bridegroom, who intends to make us his pure bride and to make his home with us forever and ever.

The Questions We Need to Have Answered

We often come to the Bible with questions we think we need to have answered and discover that the Bible presents us with answers to a completely different set of questions that we didn't know enough to ask. The Bible opens up God's agenda to us and in the process quiets our own. We come looking for answers to our questions about what we should do, and the Bible meets us with its own questions, repeatedly pointing us to what Christ has done.

Job asks how the suffering of an innocent man can be redeemed. And the answer is, by the redeemer that Job saw only in shadow but we see clearly in Jesus Christ. Job asks, "How can a man be in the right before God?" (Job 9:2). And we know, "For our sake [God] made him to be sin who knew no sin, so that in him we might become the righteousness of God" (2 Cor. 5:21). Job longs for a mediator that he cannot see

(Job 9:32). But we know "there is one mediator between God and men, the man Christ Jesus" (1 Tim. 2:5).

The psalmists ask, "Who shall ascend the hill of the LORD?" (Ps. 24:3), "Who is this King of glory?" (Ps. 24:8), and "Who is the man who fears the LORD?" (Ps. 25:12). And we know the answer. Jesus will ascend the hill of the Lord, making it possible for us to one day enter into God's holy presence. Jesus is the king of glory who reigns forever and ever. Jesus is the man who fears the Lord perfectly in our place.

Proverbs asks, "Does not wisdom call? Does not understanding raise her voice?" (8:1). And we know that in Christ "are hidden all the treasures of wisdom and knowledge" (Col. 2:3). We have heard wisdom's call in Christ's call to repent and believe.

Ecclesiastes asks, "What has a man from all the toil and striving of heart with which he toils beneath the sun?" (2:22). And we know that in him we live and move and have our being (Acts 17:28) and that nothing done for the Lord is ever wasted (1 Cor. 15:58).

The chorus in Song of Solomon asks the bride, "What is your beloved more than another beloved?" (5:9), and we celebrate that our bridegroom is more faithful, more beautiful, and that he is stronger, purer, than any other beloved, and so we throw open the door to him saying, "Come, Lord Jesus!" (Rev. 22:20).

As we work our way through the Wisdom Books of the Old Testament, we will not only understand the writings in these books more clearly because we are looking at them through the illumination of Christ, but we will also see new facets of the person and work of Christ as they are presented uniquely in Old Testament Wisdom Books. We will take in and enjoy and explore "the mystery hidden for ages and generations but now revealed to his saints" (Col. 1:26).

And we'll be grateful that we have the illumination of the entire New Testament to see Christ in the Old Testament, which the saints of the Old Testament era did not have, as well as the Holy Spirit living inside us, helping us to understand his written Word and apply it to our experiences in this world. This, indeed, is how God guides us.

The Newness We Need in Our Minds

Do you long to know God's will for your life, for your family, for today's to-do list and tomorrow's big decisions? Peter said that it comes through knowing Christ. "His divine power has granted to us all things that pertain to life and godliness, *through the knowledge of him* who called us to his own glory and excellence" (2 Pet. 1:3).

Paul also tells us how we can discern God's will. And it is not by leaving thinking and decision making behind to listen for divine messages. He wrote: "Do not be conformed to this world, but be transformed *by the renewal of your mind,* that by testing *you may discern* what is the will of God, what is good and acceptable and perfect" (Rom. 12:2).

God intends, by his Spirit through the means of the Scripture, to accomplish a metamorphosis in the way you think. He intends to make you wise, to give to you "the mind of Christ" (1 Cor. 2:16) so that you will see the way Christ sees and desire what he desires and assess the way he assesses and be repelled by what repels him.[5] He wants you to have a mind that increasingly thinks more like he thinks so that you will choose the way he chooses.

God, by uniting us to Christ by the Spirit, is filling us with "the knowledge of his will in all spiritual wisdom and understanding, so as to walk in a manner worthy of the Lord, fully pleasing to him, bearing fruit in every good work and increasing in the knowledge of God" (Col. 1:9–10). He has given us the privilege of prayer so that we might pour out our concerns and questions before him and share our lives with him in intimate and personal ways. And he has given us the Holy Spirit who illumines our reading of the Scripture so that we can understand it, apply it, and live in light of it. The Spirit takes the words on the pages of our Bible and impresses them into our minds and hearts so that we hear God speaking to us through them.

This is why you and I intend to open up our Bibles over the coming weeks to study God's Word together. As we immerse ourselves in the wisdom of the Scriptures, the Spirit will renew our minds. Wisdom from God is not a mysterious thing that is revealed to us in a secret experience of the heart. It is revealed to us in a Bible experience in which our minds are renewed and our hearts are cleansed.

God is not hiding from you what you most need to know from him. The secret wisdom, God's mysterious plan for the world, and for your life, has been fully disclosed, put on glorious display in Jesus Christ.

> Now to him who is able to strengthen you according to my gospel and the preaching of Jesus Christ, according to the revelation of the mystery that was kept secret for long ages but has now been disclosed and through the prophetic writings has been made known to all nations, according to the command of the eternal God, to bring about the obedience of faith—to the only wise God be glory forevermore through Jesus Christ! Amen. (Rom. 16:25–27)

Looking Forward: Wisdom Redeemed

When Christ returns and completes his work of redeeming all things, we will have not only redeemed and purified bodies but also redeemed and purified emotions and thoughts. Indeed, when all things are redeemed, our now faulty and often confused wisdom will be redeemed and even glorified. Salvation is God's way of restoring all things to their proper order—the way things once were in Eden. So if we want to let our minds imagine what it will be like to live in the new heaven and the new earth as one whose wisdom has been redeemed, considering the way it once was in Eden provides insight.

If we look back at Adam and Eve in the garden before the fall, we realize that they did not know everything. They learned as they experienced life in Eden where God walked with them in the cool of the day. They knew more a week after they were created than they did on their first day.[6] Likewise, we will not become omniscient at the resurrection. To be sinless does not imply that we will have nothing to learn. In fact, when we look at the only person who was ever sinless, we discover that Jesus "increased in wisdom and stature and in favor with God and man" (Luke 2:52).

Just as Adam and Eve used the freedom that God gave them within clear boundaries to make decisions, so will we, as we reign with Christ, make important decisions, devise plans, and share ideas.[7] Heaven will not be the removal of the need for wise decisions but the redemption of it. Our thoughts will no longer be plagued by sinful selfishness, prideful misconceptions, impure obsessions, or poisonous cynicism. Satan will not slip into heaven to tempt us as "nothing unclean will ever enter it, nor anyone who does what is detestable or false" (Rev. 21:27). While some of us may have thoughts that others don't, and while we may have differing perspectives, we'll be able to interact in regard to our differences in perfect love, without the blur of defensiveness or ego.

Life in the new heaven and the new earth will not be a static experience of knowing but an ongoing learning experience. It will unfold before us in ages, one new era of discovery after another, with new waves of the beauty and goodness and wisdom of God washing over us.

> By grace you have been saved—and [God] raised us up with him
> and seated us with him in the heavenly places in Christ Jesus, so
> that *in the coming ages* he might show the immeasurable riches
> of his grace in kindness toward us in Christ Jesus. (Eph. 2:5–7)

One day we will emerge from this momentary blink called human history and enter the everlasting kingdom of Christ, unfolding age upon age, each one showing us something new about God in ever clearer manifestations of his infinite wisdom. Our minds will finally and forever shake off all dullness so that with minds bright and quick we'll see everything about God with new richness of understanding and new pleasures of fascination. Our experience of him will not come from our powers of discovery but through his powers of display as he reveals more and more of himself to us.[8]

The Wisdom that formed the earth and everything in it, and ordered history and brought it about, and chose to use the foolish things of the world—like you and me—to accomplish his wise purposes, will no longer be hidden from our view but will have made his home with us.

Discussion Guide

The Wisdom Hidden in
the Wisdom Books

Getting the Discussion Going

1. Over the coming weeks we'll be studying the Psalms and Wisdom
Books together—Job, Psalms, Proverbs, Ecclesiastes, Song of Solomon.
Tell us something you remember about one of these books, or perhaps
a question you've always had about one of them.

Getting to the Heart of It

2. It is hard for those of us who have the entire Old and New Testaments to imagine what it must have been like for God's people to live
in this world and seek to follow after him without that complete written revelation. Try to put yourself in the place of God's people living in
those times. How might the teaching of the Wisdom Literature on matters such as suffering, the future of God's people, dealing with people,
finding meaning, and sexuality have been important to you?

3. Our aim as we work our way through these books is to consider what
the author of each book intended to communicate to his original audience. We also want to see what the divine author intends for us to see
in light of the fuller revelation of Christ. As the introduction offered
previews of how we will see Jesus in these Old Testament books, what
were your thoughts or reactions?

4. We read in 1 Corinthians 2:12 that Paul did not come with "lofty speech or wisdom" but was determined to "know nothing" among the Corinthians except "Jesus Christ and him crucified" in contrast to the wisdom teachers of his day who impressed the people of Corinth with philosophy and rhetoric. How is preaching the cross both incredible foolishness and infinite wisdom?

5. How does embracing the gospel and working it into your life provide the wisdom and guidance we need for life in this world?

Getting Personal

6. We've seen in this chapter that God speaks to us and guides us by his Word. Have you experienced that? Can you think of a time you would be willing to share with the group when God spoke directly to you through the Bible, giving you clear instruction?

7. Recognizing that God is in the process now of sanctifying our wisdom as he renews our minds, making it possible for us to discern what God's will is and therefore to do what is good and acceptable and perfect (Rom. 12:2), how do you think he might like to use this study of the Wisdom Literature to do that, and what is your part in it?

Getting How It Fits into the Big Picture

8. Throughout this study, we will be seeking to grasp how the passage we're studying fits into the bigger story of God's plan for redemption. The Psalms and Wisdom Books are not part of the sequence of narrative books in the Old Testament that tell us what happened next to the Israelites. Rather, they reflect the experiences, the insight, and the revelation of God that God's people turned over in their minds as they looked back at their history and forward to their future. With what you know at this point about the Psalms and Wisdom Books, what do they add to our understanding of how God is working out his plan to redeem all things?

Week 2

Job

Personal Bible Study

Job

Even though it is not the first book in our Bible, Job may actually have been the first book of the Bible written, though we don't know who wrote it or exactly when it was written. Job is a story or drama about a real person in a real place (Uz, which is southeast of Israel), who lived at a particular time in history, probably between the time of Abraham and that of Moses. Job was likely not a descendant of Abraham like most of the key characters in the Old Testament were, but was more likely a gentile who embraced God's covenant promises similar to Caleb, Jethro, Rahab, Ruth, and Naaman.

1. Read Job 1:1–5. What does the writer of this book seem to want us to understand about Job?

2. Read Job 1:6–11. How would you paraphrase Satan's argument against God?

3. Read Job 1:12. Notice that Satan has asked for permission to harm Job and that God has granted that permission along with setting some parameters for Job's suffering. What do you think this says about Satan and ultimately about God?

4. Read Job 1:13–2:10. How is Job's response to incredible suffering so far quite different from the way Satan said Job would respond in 1:11 and 2:5?

In chapter 2, we read that Job had three friends who traveled to where he lived just to comfort him, and when they saw what had happened to him, they "raised their voices and wept" (v. 12). They sat with him silently for seven days, and then they couldn't stay silent any longer. In chapters 3–37, we have three rounds of impassioned debate between Job and his three friends, later joined by a fourth friend, as they focus on the question of what Job's suffering reveals both about him and about God's governing of the world.

The book of Job doesn't dismiss Job's friends as hypocrites or heretics. In fact, each believes firmly in the one God who is not only all-powerful but wholly just and, at the same time, quick to restore the penitent and to heap blessings on the teachable. Yet both Job (16:2) and God (42:7–9) deem them "miserable comforters." "The basic error of Job's friends is that they overestimate their grasp of truth, misapply the truth they know, and close their minds to any facts that contradict what they assume."[1]

5. You may want to read chapters 3–37 if you never have before. Or you may want only to skim these chapters, utilizing the chapter titles in your Bible to develop a general sense of the flow and content of the arguments. As you read or skim, write down some key phrases or questions from the chapters along with your own impressions about what you observe about Job and his friends.

6. A key question is voiced by Eliphaz in 4:17: "Can mortal man be in the right before God? Can a man be pure before his Maker?" Job expresses something similar in 9:1–2. How does Job's question differ from his friend's question?

7. Last week we learned that the Wisdom Books raise questions that can only be answered in Jesus Christ. How is that the case with this key question (question 6)?

8. Job longs for God to vindicate his integrity, but he knows he can't forge the gap between himself and God; he longs for an intermediary who can make this happen (9:33; 16:19–21; 19:25–27). How is this longing fulfilled only in Jesus?

Finally, after all of these speeches, God himself speaks from out of a whirlwind in chapters 38–41. Read through these chapters, noting a phrase or two along with its reference about:

∽ God's wisdom in creation:

∽ God's wisdom in executing justice:

∽ God's wisdom in the use of his power:

9. How does what God has to say in the storm answer or not answer all that has been said about him in the previous chapters?

10. Job 40:3–5 and 42:1–6 record Job's response to hearing God speak from the storm. Write down phrases or ideas from these verses that reveal the following responses from Job:

∽ Submission:

~ Humility:

~ Repentance:

11. Job's restoration is almost like a resurrection. He has been reconciled with his friends and is given double portions of everything he had before except that he is given only ten more children rather than twenty children. How might this detail alone perhaps hint to us that Job's story is meant to point us toward anticipation of resurrection?

12. How does Job point us to Christ as a type of Christ both through comparison and contrast? Read the observation and quote from Job in the first column and write down a statement of similarity or contrast to Christ in the second column as indicated by the reference following the example provided in the first one.

Job	Jesus
Job was "blameless and upright, one who feared God and turned away from evil." (Job 1:1)	Heb. 4:15 *Jesus was "without sin."*
God used even the work of Satan for his own glory and for Job's sanctification. (Job 2:6)	Acts 2:23
Job's misery was increased by the friends who came around him. (Job 16:1)	Matt. 26: 40, 43, 56; Mark 14:66–68
Job bemoaned, "Men have gaped at me with their mouth; they have struck me insolently on the cheek; they mass themselves together against me. God gives me up to the ungodly and casts me into the hands of the wicked" (Job 16:10–11); and, "Sure there are mockers about me. . . . I am the one before whom men spit." (Job 17:2, 6)	Matt. 26:67; 27:29, 31, 41

Job said: "I will give free utterance to my complaint. I will speak in the bitterness of my soul" (Job 10:1); and "I will defend my integrity until I die." (Job 27:5 NLT)	Matt. 27:12; Mark 14:61
Job determined to put his hope in God *even if* God killed him. (Job 13:15)	Matt. 26:38–39
Job's hopes were centered in resurrection, saying, "After my skin has been thus destroyed, yet in my flesh I shall see God." (Job 19:26)	Luke 9:22
Job submitted to God in his suffering. (Job 42:1–6)	Heb. 5:7–10
Job prayed for his friends, and God forgave them. (Job 42:10)	Luke 23:34

13. In the second column below, record how the book of Job also points to Christ in the way that Christ answers its unanswered questions, meets its unfilled needs, and brings about its anticipated restoration and resurrection. An answer is provided for the first one to serve as an example.

Job	*Jesus*
Finding no meaning or purpose in his suffering, Job asks, "Why is light given to him who is in misery, and life to the bitter in soul?" (Job 3:20)	Phil. 3:8–10 *Knowing Christ gives meaning to our suffering as it gives us an opportunity to share in his sufferings.*
Eliphaz asks, "Who that was innocent ever perished?" (Job 4:7)	Luke 23:47
Job asks, "What is man, that you make so much of him, and that you set your heart on him?" (Job 7:17)	Heb. 2:6, 10

Job asks, "Why do you not pardon my transgression and take away my iniquity?" (Job 7:21)	Matt. 26:28
Bildad asks, "Does God pervert justice?" (Job 8:3)	Rom. 3:23–26
Job longed for an "arbiter" or "mediator" between himself and God. (Job 9:14, 33)	1 Tim. 2:5, 1 John 2:1–2
Job wonders if God can sympathize at all with his suffering, asking him, "Have you eyes of flesh? Do you see as man sees?" (Job 10:4)	Heb. 4:15
Job asks, "If a man dies, shall he live again?" (Job 14:14)	John 5:24–25
Job believes he has an intercessor, saying, "Even now, behold, my witness is in heaven, and he who testifies for me is on high." (Job 16:19)	Rom. 8:34
Job wonders if the best he can hope for is the grave, asking, "Where then is my hope? . . . Will it go down to the bars of Sheol?" (Job 17:15–16)	1 Cor. 15:19–20, 54
Job says, "For I know that my Redeemer lives, and at the last he will stand upon the earth. And after my skin has been thus destroyed, yet in my flesh I shall see God." (Job 19:25–26)	1 Cor. 15:20–23; Rev. 22:4
Job asks, "But where shall wisdom be found? And where is the place of understanding?" (Job 28:12)	1 Cor. 1:30; Col. 2:3

Teaching Chapter

No Fair

I can remember doing my part before dinner when I was a child, filling up glasses with Kool-Aid to put on the table, doing my best to dole out perfectly even amounts of the sugary, colored goodness, knowing that if I gave myself more than my brother or sister, that great cry of childhood injustices would ring out: "No fair!"

She got more than I did. No fair. I shouldn't have to do this. No fair. I deserve to get one. No fair.

Oh how we long for fairness—expect it, even demand it. We see ourselves as experts on what is fair and what is clearly not fair at all. And this is not just childhood immaturity. We spend our lives looking for fairness—if not from our parents and siblings, teachers and coaches, bosses and coworkers, at least we want and expect it from God.

Recently I received a letter from a man who told me that all three of his adult children gave birth to babies around the same time, but one of the babies had been diagnosed with a fatal disease and would likely not see his first birthday. He wrote:

> Our daughter and her wonderful husband are really struggling with the fairness of all this. The other two of our three adult children have had children out of wedlock. Our daughter and her husband have been the ones with the strong faith. There were many times she and her now husband were tempted to give into their desires before they were married, but they did not because they desired to be obedient to God in the area of purity.

But now she has been questioning God, asking, *Why us? We are the ones who waited. My siblings who did not wait—they are the ones with the healthy children, and we are the ones with a child who has been given a death sentence!*

We have a sense of how we think things work with God: *I identify myself with him, and he uses his power to provide me with protection from the hard things that happen to people. If I am good, he will give me a life that is good.* And when life doesn't work out that way for us we are quick to cry out to God, "No fair!"

> *Perhaps the book of Job is in the Bible not to answer all our questions about suffering but to reframe our questions with its profound wisdom.*

As we start our journey through the Wisdom Books, beginning in the ancient book of Job, we discover that our way of looking at life with God and what we can expect from God as one who belongs to him hasn't changed very much from those who lived in ancient times. The cry of Job in the face of unimaginable suffering is "No fair!"

This grandfather who wrote me the letter says that he was "finding it very difficult to not question God and his plan." He said that he was afraid Satan would use this seeming unfairness to make his daughter bitter toward God. And certainly we know that often happens. Do you know some people who once walked with God but who have since walked away from him because they feel he has not done right by them? Why is it that so many people end up angry and alienated from God when hard things happen to them? Perhaps it's because they had unmet expectations based on assumptions about who God is and the nature of his job in the universe—especially in regard to the lives of those he claims as his own.

If you see it as my job to water your flowers and assume that because I'm your neighbor I will water your flowers, and I don't water your flowers and instead your flowers die, you might be angry with me. But your anger toward me would be unjustified, because I never promised to water your flowers (just look at my flowerbed to know that I don't water my own flowers!). You need to check your assumptions.

The book of Job, for its ancient as well as modern readers, challenges our assumptions about how we think this life with God in regard to suffering ought to work. This is wisdom for those who live in a world in which people who belong to God suffer. Perhaps the book of Job is in the Bible not to answer all our questions about suffering but to reframe our questions with its profound wisdom. And to absorb its wisdom, we need to allow it to confront our incorrect assumptions.

In the first verse and paragraph of the book of Job, we learn that Job is a good man, a great man in fact, and more than that, a godly man.

> There was a man in the land of Uz whose name was Job, and that man was blameless and upright, one who feared God and turned away from evil. There were born to him seven sons and three daughters. He possessed 7,000 sheep, 3,000 camels, 500 yoke of oxen, and 500 female donkeys, and very many servants, so that this man was the greatest of all the people of the east. His sons used to go and hold a feast in the house of each one on his day, and they would send and invite their three sisters to eat and drink with them. And when the days of the feast had run their course, Job would send and consecrate them, and he would rise early in the morning and offer burnt offerings according to the number of them all. For Job said, "It may be that my children have sinned, and cursed God in their hearts." Thus Job did continually. (Job 1:1–5)

Job is a great man morally; he turns away from evil. He is a great man personally with what appears to be the perfect family. He is a great man financially with tremendous wealth and holdings. And he is a great man spiritually, evidenced by his great sensitivity to sin against a holy God.

What difference does it make that Job was a great man? Why does the writer want us to know that? Because he knows it will prompt us to say, "He doesn't deserve this."

Assumption 1: If I Am Godly, I Won't Have to Suffer

We have this sensibility that tells us if we do the right things, if we go to church and are generous to others, if we are clearly on God's team, then we will somehow, or should somehow, be spared from significant suffering. But as we look at Job, we see, contrary to our sense of justice or fairness, that goodness and godliness are no guarantee that we will not have to suffer. We have an underlying equation about the way we think things ought to work: My good behavior and spiritual intentions + God's love and power = a life in which things go well for me.

Interestingly Job's goodness and godliness work in his life in the opposite way from what we might expect. Instead of exempting him from suffering, they seem to make him the prime candidate for it:

> And the LORD said to Satan, "Have you considered my servant Job, that there is none like him on the earth, a blameless and upright man, who fears God and turns away from evil?" Then Satan answered the LORD and said, "Does Job fear God for no reason? Have you not put a hedge around him and his house and all that he has, on every side? You have blessed the work of his hands, and his possessions have increased in the land. But stretch out your hand and touch all that he has, and he will curse you to your face." (Job 1:8–11)

Satan comes before God in an attempt to diminish and humiliate God, saying that none of God's people really love him for himself but solely for what they can get from him. He suggests that Job is in a relationship with God only because he is supernaturally protected by God and has been given such a comfortable life by God. He says if Job's comfortable life were to be taken away, Job would turn on God.

That is the big question that drives this whole story. Will Job reject God when trouble comes, or will he be faithful to God no matter what, proving Satan's accusation to be false?

Satan certainly has insight into human nature. He recognizes that if you are in relationship with God solely for what you can get from him, at the first sign that you're not getting what you want, what you think you've been promised, your suffering will sink what you've called "faith." If you came to God because someone told you that "God loves you and has a wonderful plan for your life," assuming that means that God's job is to give you the comfortable, pain-free life of fulfillment you have always dreamed of, then you will likely forsake faith at the first sign of adversity.

God does not promise his children that we will not have to suffer.

In fact, the Bible tells believers over and over that we should expect to suffer.

Let's consider some of the most godly people we see in Scripture. There is Abraham, whom God chose to be the father of his people. Imagine Abraham's suffering during all those years waiting for a son and then as he walked up the mountain preparing to sacrifice that beloved son on an altar. There is David, who was described as "a man after God's own heart." Imagine David's suffering as he ran from cave to cave in a desperate attempt to elude the murderous intentions of Saul and, later, his own son. Think of John the Baptist, about whom Jesus said, "Among those born of women there has arisen no one greater" (Matt. 11:11). Imagine John the Baptist's suffering as he languished in prison questioning if Jesus was really the Messiah and then as he faced being beheaded.

But, most significantly, let's look at Jesus—the most innocent person who ever lived, who suffered more physically, emotionally, and spiritually than any person who has ever lived. By taking it on himself, Jesus dignified human suffering. Of all the kinds of lives he could have lived, he chose a life of suffering. Because we know the goodness of Jesus, and that he was, in fact, God in the flesh, we can never say that if we are good enough and godly enough, we will not have to suffer.

For Job, a godly and good man, the suffering came down hard, ripping away from him everything he owned and nearly everyone he loved. All of his property was destroyed and all of his children were killed when the house in which they were having a dinner party collapsed on them. Then Satan struck again, going even deeper by taking away Job's health so that Job ended up sitting outside the city on the ash heap, or garbage heap, scraping the dead skin from his oozing sores that covered him from head to toe, wishing he had never been born.

Most people think of the book of Job as a book about Job's suffering. And if we had only an account of his suffering and struggle, we might think that too. But the narrator of Job's story puts the story in context for us so that we are privy to the spiritual realities going on behind the scenes. This allows us to see that this story is about much more than Job's suffering; it's about God's glory. It is not merely a story about something happening on this earth but about something happening in heaven.

> Now there was a day when the sons of God came to present themselves before the LORD, and Satan also came among them. The LORD said to Satan, "From where have you come?" Satan answered the LORD and said, "From going to and fro on the earth, and from walking up and down on it." (Job 1:6–7)

Satan has come before God in heaven, along with all of the other inhabitants of the spiritual realities beyond what we can see, to bring an accusation against God. He asserts that God is not worthy of being loved by humans apart from the good gifts he gives to them in the here and now. And God responds by telling Satan to look down at the land of Uz where he will find a man who will trust and love him no matter what suffering Satan inflicts on him.

> And the LORD said to Satan, "Behold, all that he has is in your hand. Only against him do not stretch out your hand." So Satan went out from the presence of the LORD. (Job 1:12)

Wait a minute, we want to say. That's not fair. Poor Job is down there completely unaware of what is going on, and he's about to have the sky fall in on his life. Satan has asked permission to harm Job, and God has given the permission.

This just doesn't fit with our assumptions of what a loving, protecting God should do for one of his own, does it? But it is clear. God gives the permission and sets the parameters for Job's suffering. He says basically, "Okay, you can put him to the test. But you can only go this far." This reveals something very important about Satan, and ultimately about God.

Satan has to ask permission from God because Satan has no power that is not given to him by God. You know God is powerful, and you believe that God is more powerful than Satan, right? But the bigger truth is that Satan has absolutely no power that has not been granted to him by God. That is how sovereign God is over the universe. And that is how limited Satan is in the world. Although, right now, Satan has been given a very long leash to use the power that God has granted to him. But the day is coming when that will end.

The book of Job shows us that not everything that happens in our lives can be explained in terms of the reality that we see and know in the here and now, which addresses our second false assumption.

Assumption 2: My Suffering Is about Me and My Life in the Here and Now

If we allow the Bible to define reality for us, we realize that everything that happens in our lives is not ultimately about us.

> For we do not wrestle against flesh and blood, but against the rulers, against the authorities, against the cosmic powers over this present darkness, against the spiritual forces of evil in the heavenly places. (Eph. 6:12)

The writer of the book of Job pulls back the curtain on the ultimate reality beyond what we can see in the natural world and allows us to see the supernatural battle behind the scenes in Job's suffering. In the Gospel of Luke, Jesus does the same thing, revealing the supernatural battle behind the scenes in the life of Simon Peter.

> Simon, Simon, behold, Satan demanded to have you, that he might sift you like wheat, but I have prayed for you that your faith may not fail. And when you have turned again, strengthen your brothers. (Luke 22:31–32)

Satan had a destructive purpose in Job's suffering: to *destroy* Job's trust in the God he loved. But God also had a purpose in giving Satan permission to harm Job: to *develop* Job's trust in the God he loved.

Likewise, Satan had a destructive purpose in Peter's sifting: to *destroy* his relationship to Christ and disqualify him from serving Christ's church. And likewise, God also had a purpose in giving Satan permission to sift Peter: to *develop* Peter's love for Christ and his usefulness in the body of Christ.

Yet ultimately, in both cases, Satan's destructive purposes were about something far more than harming Job or Peter. They were just pawns to him in his determination to defeat and diminish God. Satan intended to bring Job to the place where he would curse God to his face, and Satan intended to bring Peter to the place that he would deny Christ. Satan intended that both incidents would serve as a demonstration that would diminish God. But God, in his sovereignty over Satan and suffering, intended for the steadfastness of Job and the restoration of Peter to be a demonstration of his glorious grace.

Yet it was not in Job's or Peter's suffering that Satan exerted his destructive intentions most profoundly. And neither was it in Job's or Peter's faithfulness or faithlessness that God's glory in suffering was most prominently put on display.

As Jesus prepared to face the cross, and as the reality of the suffering that was ahead for him began to press in on him, Jesus lifted up his eyes to heaven and said, "Father, the hour has come; glorify your Son that the Son may glorify you" (John 17:1).

Satan put it into the heart of Judas to betray Jesus. He filled the hearts of the religious leaders with jealousy and hatred so that they demanded his crucifixion. He filled the people's hearts with evil so that they lied about him, mocked him, spit on him, beat him, condemned him. Satan anticipated that this would be his finest hour, when he would finally defeat God and bring him to open shame. He didn't realize that he was actually helping to accomplish the plan of God that would bring about his own destruction (Heb. 2:14), the "secret and hidden wisdom of God, which God decreed before the ages" (1 Cor. 2:7).

In his sovereignty over Satan, God purposed to use the suffering Satan inflicted on his own Son to accomplish his good purposes in the world. It is only when we see that God could actually use the immense suffering of the Son of God hanging on a cross to accomplish the great good of the salvation of sinners that we can begin to believe that God could use the unexplainable suffering in our own lives for his good purposes.

If God has given permission for your trust in him to be put to the test of suffering, let the wisdom of Job inform your response to it, recognizing that your life is about much more than the here and now, and about more than your own concerns and comfort. God intends for you to be a living demonstration of his magnificent glory as you rest in him, even when you can't understand or explain him. Not only that, but he intends to share his glory with all who are willing to share his suffering (Rom. 8:17). As Peter, the sifted one, later wrote: "Rejoice insofar as you share Christ's sufferings, that you may also rejoice and be glad when his glory is revealed" (1 Pet. 4:13).

Assumption 3: My Suffering Is the Result of God's Punishing Me for My Sin

While you and I as readers know from the first chapter of Job that Job has turned away from evil and that God himself has said Job is blameless, and while we are privy to the wager with which Satan has challenged God, Job's friends do not have that advantage. And as they circle around Job in his suffering state, they are quite certain they know the cause of Job's incredible suffering: Job's suffering is Job's fault. Job is being punished for some secret sin. In fact, according to Zophar, Job is not simply getting what he deserves but less than he deserves. He says to Job, "Know then that God exacts of you less that your guilt deserves" (Job 11:6). Job's friends assume that this kind of extreme suffering comes only to someone who has committed a heinous sin that God has determined must be punished.

And we get this assumption, don't we? We assume that in our suffering, God is punishing us.

When we read the book of Job, we realize this assumption must come to us humans quite naturally since it is as ancient as this story and still seems to be our default setting. Who has not experienced something that caused them to think, *Finally, what I've done has caught up with me, and now God is making me pay?*

I remember some of my first thoughts as I awakened in the hospital the morning after we received the diagnosis that my two-day-old daughter would live less than a year. I thought, *This is my fault.*

Have you had those same kinds of thoughts when something hard happened in your life? Did you think your miscarriage or your infertility was God's way of making you pay for sexual sin or perhaps an abortion? Have you thought that God took something away from you to make you pay for loving it too much? Do you sometimes find yourself waiting for the other shoe to drop, wondering when you are going to get what you think, deep down, you really deserve?

Is that how it works? Does God punish us with suffering for the things we've done or failed to do?

My friend, if you belong to Christ, you can be confident that your suffering is not punishment for your sin. And how do I know that? *Because someone has already been punished for your sin so that you won't have to be.*

All the punishment you deserve for your sin—your outright rebellion against God or your utter apathy toward God, your refusal to love him with all of your heart, soul, mind, and strength, all of the ugliest, most shameful things you have said and done—it has all been laid on Jesus. He was punished for your sin so you won't have to be.

> But he was wounded for our transgressions;
>   he was crushed for our iniquities;
> upon him was the chastisement that brought us peace,
>   and with his stripes we are healed. (Isa. 53:5)

That is the gospel. And it goes against our instincts. It seems too good to be true. Jesus has endured the punishment you deserve and offered to you in its place his own perfect record of righteousness so that you will be showered with the love and honor from God that Christ deserves. When you hide yourself in the person of Jesus, you don't have to fear that God is going to take out his anger on you. He poured out the punishment that you rightly deserve on his own Son so that he can pour out something quite different on you, something you don't deserve and could never earn. God intends to pour out his love, his mercy, his grace, and his forgiveness on you.

If you are in Christ, you can be sure that your suffering is not divine punishment for your sin. Rather than divine punishment, isn't much of the suffering we experience actually the natural result of living in a world in which the curse of sin has taken root and infected everything? And certainly some of our suffering is simply experiencing the natural consequences of our sinful choices and the sinful choices of others.

There's a difference between enduring divine punishment and experiencing the natural consequences of our choices, isn't there?

Most significantly, as a child of God we can be confident that whenever we suffer, no matter the cause, God intends to use it to discipline us for our good. The writer of Hebrews tells us that "the Lord disciplines the one he loves" and that "for the moment all discipline seems painful rather than pleasant" (Heb.12:6, 11). Obviously, discipline doesn't feel good at the time; it feels like hardship, and loss, and pain. What allows us as his children to endure it is that while it's painful, we're confident it's purposeful. Never punitive. Never random. Never too harsh. Always out of love. What is that divine purpose? God's desire is that "it yields the peaceful fruit of righteousness to those who have been trained by it" (Heb.12:11). Your suffering, in the hands of your loving Father, becomes a tool that he intends to use to make you fruitful. Fruitfulness requires pruning, and pruning usually hurts. But pruning is purposeful, not punitive. God intends to prune you so that your life will be full of the abundant blessings of living in wisdom.

We are glad to know our suffering is purposeful and not random or meaningless. But mostly we just want it to end, which leads to our fourth false assumption.

Assumption 4: What I Need Most from God Are Relief for My Suffering and Answers to My Questions

So many suffering people get stuck demanding an answer they can understand and articulate to the question "Why?" The problem is that God does not promise to provide us with a specific reason for the suffering in our lives (assuming we could understand it if he did) other than that he intends to conform us to the image of his Son (Rom. 8:29). He has promised that he has a purpose in it, and he calls us to trust him with that purpose—to believe in what we can't see, which is the essence of faith (John 20:29; Heb. 11:1).

Throughout most of the chapters of Job, Job is waiting for some answers. He listened to all of the arguments and explanations from his friends as to why he was suffering and argued his case with them. But he wanted to argue his case before God and to hear from God. He wanted

God to show up and testify on his behalf, making it clear that he did not, indeed, have some secret sin that had brought all of this calamity upon him. "Let the Almighty answer me," he says in Job 31:35.

And finally, after all the questioning and struggle, in a voice from out of a storm, God spoke.

Now, what we might expect, when God finally spoke, is that God would set everyone straight on the fine points of why this has happened and what he is doing. We might think God would tell Job all about Satan's scheme to diminish him by exposing that Job was only interested in God for what he could get from him. But when God finally spoke, rather than revealing all of the answers to Job's questions or explaining the spiritual battle going on behind the scenes, God revealed himself. Rather than telling Job what he might have wanted most to hear, he told Job what he needed most to hear.

God began by asking where Job was when God began the work of creation, revealing himself as creator. His phrases are "Where were you when? Can you do this? Do you know how?" As God revealed himself, the message became clear to Job: *God is Creator and I am the created. He can do anything with me that he wants to do with me.*

These questions go on for two chapters until, at the beginning of chapter 40, it's as if God took a breath and started again. Job had suggested that he had been treated unfairly, and in God's questions, God responded to Job's complaint about the lack of justice in his suffering somewhat indirectly, challenging Job to take on the characteristics of deity to administer justice in the universe.

We like to think that we are the experts on justice—that we have the ability to determine what is fair and right in this world. But when God reveals himself to us, when we truly see him, we see the true, perfect, pure justice of God, and we realize that we don't begin to have the wisdom and perspective to judge what is right. Instead we see that God in his innate nature is the plumb line of justice that all justice is judged against. As God reveals himself, Job realizes: *God is a righteous judge, and I have limited understanding. He will always do what is right with me.*

God knew that Job needed to hear something more significant than answers to his questions to move toward healing. God knew that the more

Job understood about the character, the power, and the purposes of God, the more Job could trust him without having all of his questions answered.

You may feel that you have questions that need to be answered about the reason for your pain or what purpose God has in it. But what you need even more is for God to reveal himself to you in an unmistakable, unavoidable way so that you can see him as he is, not as a religion has portrayed him or as a book has described him, but as he truly is in all of his wisdom and glory and power and perfection. What you really need is for him to change the course of the conversation.

> *The wisdom of God ... moves us from demanding from God what we think we deserve to thanking God for all that we've received that we do not deserve.*

This is what happened to Job. And when God revealed himself to Job, Job came to realize that the more he knew about *who God is*, the more he could accept *what God gave*—even when he didn't understand it.

I think Job would say that, in the storms of his life, he finally realized that there was something he needed more than having his questions answered and his suffering relieved and even his reputation restored. He needed to see the character and glory of God more clearly and powerfully. He needed to see God's glory at the center of everything, not his own comfort. He needed to see that God does not settle for our small ideas of what he should be doing in the world.

The wisdom of God, the revelation of God that thunders from out of the whirlwind, quiets our questions; it humbles our great claims of expertise in regard to what is fair and right. It moves us from demanding from God what we think we deserve to thanking God for all that we've received that we do not deserve.

As the wisdom and perspective we discover in the book of Job begins to sink in, instead of telling God, "I don't deserve this!" when hard things happen, we begin to say, "I don't deserve anything good you've ever given me. I don't deserve to have you in my life. Every drop of goodness I've known and experienced in my life flows out of your goodness. You know better than I what is right and good for me."

On the surface, a perfectly fair world appeals to us. But it is not really fairness we need from God. In a completely fair world, there would be no room for the grace that is ours in Jesus Christ—receiving what we don't deserve. And there would be no room for mercy either—being spared from getting the punishment we do deserve. We deserve punishment but receive forgiveness; we deserve rejection but experience love; we deserve judgment but are showered with God's mercy; we deserve to die but are given unending life. It's simply not fair, but it is so very, very good.

Looking Forward: My Redeemer Lives

After Satan struck Job with "loathsome sores from the sole of his foot to the crown of his head," Job's sores were open and oozing pus and became infested with maggots or worms, and his skin turned black (Job 7:5; 30:30). Job's loathsome state required that he relocate from his home to the town ash heap, the place outside the city where its rubbish was burned and where people with skin diseases were sent.

Death began to loom large in Job's mind, having given up any hope of God's answering his cry for vindication. At first, Job's vision of the future life was obscure, and we hear him asking the hopeful question, "If a man dies, shall he live again? All the days of my service I would wait, till my renewal should come" (Job 14:14). Somewhere along the way, as Job pursued God in the agony of his suffering, God revealed the answer to Job so that he was able to speak of resurrection life with firm confidence:

> For I know that my Redeemer lives,
>   and at the last he will stand upon the earth.
> And after my skin has been thus destroyed,
>   yet in my flesh I shall see God,
> whom I shall see for myself,
>   and my eyes shall behold, and not another.
> My heart faints within me! (Job 19:25–27)

The Hebrew word translated "Redeemer" is *go'el*, and it had two general applications. It was used to refer to the next of kin who intervened to maintain the rights or preserve the continuity of the family (as it is used in the book of Ruth referring to Boaz). But in daily usage, its primary meaning was "one who restores" or "one who puts something back into its original or pristine condition." This is the prophetic vision Job had of Jesus himself—his restorer, his redeemer.

Job envisioned a day when his *go'el* will restore his long-dead body and remake it into a body fit for the new heaven and the new earth where the Redeemer will live with redeemed humanity. Job longed for the day when he will gaze with his eyes upon his God-Redeemer standing "upon the earth." It was not the thought of his soul resting with God in a far-off heaven that brought him such intense anticipation, but the thought of seeing God in glorified flesh standing in victory on a renewed earth.

God gave Job the prophetic ability to see not the first coming of Christ but the second coming, when "the Lord himself will descend from heaven with a cry of command" (1 Thess. 4:16). He could see with eyes of faith the renewal that Paul described when he wrote:

> Our earthly bodies are planted in the ground when we die, but they will be raised to live forever. Our bodies are buried in brokenness, but they will be raised in glory. They are buried in weakness, but they will be raised in strength. (1 Cor. 15:42–43 NLT)

And so we too look toward the resurrection. We look beyond the ash heap of our current suffering and beyond the confines of the grave to the day when all those who are in Christ will have exactly what Job's aching heart longed for. Even after our physical bodies have become dust in the ground or turned into ashes, we will be resurrected, glorified, so that our eyes will behold our blessed Redeemer.

Discussion Guide

Job

Getting the Discussion Going

1. Some of us wonder how we would respond if the worst thing we can imagine were to happen to us, and some of us already know, because the worst thing we can imagine has already happened to us. What are some of the ways people respond to incredible loss and suffering?

Getting to the Heart of It

2. Often when someone suffers we say, "She doesn't deserve that." What does that statement reveal about our assumptions about goodness and godliness in relation to suffering?

3. In this challenge between God and Job, what would define a "win" for Satan? How about for God? For Job?

4. God gives Satan permission to harm Job. What does this reveal about Satan and about God?

5. In Job 13:15, Job says, "Though he slay me, I will hope in him; yet I will argue my ways to his face." How is this a direct answer to the wager between God and Satan that began this drama?

6. When God finally answers out of the whirlwind, his entire reply is a stream of unanswerable questions. God has clearly changed the subject. It becomes clear that Job and his friends not only have the wrong answers but have been asking the wrong questions. There is nothing soothing or explanatory in these chapters. Instead, how would you characterize God's response?

7. At the beginning of Job's story we feel sorry for Job as he appears to be the unwitting victim of Satan's efforts to prove that no one loves God for who he is apart from the gifts he gives. When you read Job's response after God has revealed himself to him in the whirlwind, do you sense that God has used the suffering in Job's life for any good purpose? If so, what is it? And do you think it was worth the suffering he experienced?

Getting Personal

8. Throughout the book of Job, we see Job vacillate between despair and hope, between confusion and clarity. Can you relate to that from your own experiences of suffering?

Getting How It Fits into the Big Picture

9. Job's righteousness had to have come about through his faith in God's promise of a savior as expressed in Genesis 3:15 in whatever form and with whatever additional information Job may have been taught. Whatever he knew of the history of redemption, it would seem that Job was clinging specifically and explicitly to some promise or affirmation from God (Job 6:10). Somewhere along the line Job had been convinced that God had spoken a promise of grace and that he could stand on those words with full assurance. His faith had content (words) and was not just whistling-in-the-dark wishful thinking, and yet his understanding of how God would provide salvation to him was not as clear as ours is because we have the entire Old and New Testaments. Looking back at the two charts you filled out in regard to the various ways the book of Job points to Christ, which were particularly meaningful to you?

Week 3

Psalms: The Songs of Jesus

Psalms: The Songs of Jesus

How does the created speak to the Creator? How does a sinner cry out for mercy before a holy God? How does a sufferer lay out a complaint against a just God? How does a needy human lay out his or her needs before the Shepherd? The Psalms show us how. Because, while we hear the voice of God speaking to us through most of the Bible, the Psalms speak in a human voice, providing us with divinely inspired poetry to express our hearts and minds to God.

The Psalms are an honest expression of emotions, while at the same time they help us to discipline our emotions. They teach us that our emotions are grounded in our covenant faith, contradicting our mistaken belief that emotions are something over which we have no control.

1. Read each of the quotes from the Psalms in the first column and identify the emotion the psalmist is expressing to God, writing it down in the second column.

"You have put more joy in my heart than they have when their grain and wine abound." (Ps. 4:7)	Joy that flows from a heart that rests in God.
"In peace I will both lie down and sleep." (Ps. 4:8)	The "peace of God" which "passes all understanding"
"I will bow down toward your holy temple in the fear of you." (Ps. 5:7)	Reverence and awe for a Holy God.

"Make them bear their guilt, O God." (Ps. 5:10)	
"My eye wastes away because of grief." (Ps. 6:7)	Sorrow and lamentation
"I will be glad and exult in you." (Ps. 9:2)	Rejoicing in and exulting because of Christ.
"My heart shall rejoice in your salvation." (Ps. 13:5)	Jubilation and thankfulness for God the Redeemer.
"I love you, O LORD, my strength." (Ps. 18:1)	Love and adoration for Christ.
"In your salvation how greatly he exults." (Ps. 21:1)	Acknowledging the salvation of God and glorying in that Salvation.
"I am lonely and afflicted." (Ps. 25:16)	feelings of isolation, pain, and sorrow.
"Though war arise against me, yet I will be confident." (Ps. 27:3)	Unshakable faith in God who is "Our refuge and Strength"
"My life is spent with sorrow." (Ps. 31:10)	Anguish, grief, and broken
"Let your steadfast love, O LORD, be upon us, even as we hope in you." (Ps. 33:22)	
"The LORD is near to the brokenhearted and saves the crushed in spirit." (Ps. 34:18)	
"I will thank you in the great congregation." (Ps. 35:18)	
"I am sorry for my sin." (Ps. 38:18)	
"Why are you cast down, O my soul, and why are you in turmoil within me?" (Ps. 42:5)	
"All day long my disgrace is before me, and shame has covered my face." (Ps. 44:15)	
"A broken and contrite heart, O God, you will not despise." (Ps. 51:17)	
"Zeal for your house has consumed me." (Ps. 69:9)	
"All in vain have I kept my heart clean and washed my hands in innocence." (Ps. 73:13)	
"I am afflicted and in pain." (Ps. 69:29)	
"This is the LORD's doing; it is marvelous in our eyes." (Ps. 118:23)	

The psalms were a part of the ordinary life of the Israelites, and an integral part of Israel's worship, both corporate and individual. Some psalms began as works of private devotion, while others were designed for the purpose of public worship. In the end, however, the psalms always lead people to the worship of the living God. Psalms reveal not only the agony of the human soul but also revealed truth about our covenant God.

Development

The psalms were written by a number of different people and were a work in progress for a long time, continually being added to. We can think of the book of Psalms being "constructed," similar to the way great cathedrals took shape. Most cathedrals were built over several centuries with new sections being added over time. And while there was diversity in what was added, it all became part of a unified whole. The same is true of the Psalter. Like a cathedral, it was not constructed all in one decade or even in one century but over a one-thousand-year time period. It includes a psalm associated with Moses, and another psalm that was clearly written after the time of exile. Within the whole are recognizable smaller groupings such as the Egyptian Hallel (Psalms 113–118), which focuses on the theme of deliverance and the exodus event and was used in celebrating Passover; and the Songs of Ascents (Psalms 120–134), which are pilgrim psalms sung by people on their way to the feasts at Jerusalem.

Because it was built up over time does not make Psalms any less inspired than the books of the Bible written by a single individual. The same God who inspired Moses to write the Pentateuch and Paul to write his letters also inspired a multiplicity of authors as they wrote the psalms. And just as each psalm was composed by inspiration, so was their arrangement into a book inspired, brought together by divine design.

Genre

When we think through the various kinds of literature in the Bible, we realize that there are letters (such as Romans or Philippians), historical narrative (such as Genesis and the Gospels), prophecy (such as Isaiah and Amos) and Apocalyptic (such as Daniel and Revelation). And while there are other poetic books in the Bible, the psalms are unique in their genre of Hebrew musical poetry.

Poetry is addressed to the mind through the heart.[1] It engages us differently from a straightforward statement of fact or imperative and sometimes leaves matters ambiguous. Poetry can involve hyperbole, exaggeration, and imagery, as well as all kinds of anthropomorphisms, metaphors, and similes that we should not try to read in a strictly literal sense. In Psalms mountains skip like rams (Ps. 114:4), enemies spew out swords from their lips (Ps. 59:7), and God is portrayed as shepherd, fortress, shield, and rock. So when we read the psalms we have to carefully consider the metaphors being used, seeking to understand what they signify.

2. The psalms are intended to appeal to the emotions, to evoke feelings rather than propositional thinking, and to stimulate a response that goes beyond simply understanding facts. Why do you think God in his wisdom might have chosen to put this large portion of scriptural truth in poetic form?

Authorship

The psalms are mostly associated with David, particularly in the early portion of the Psalter, and he is known as the "sweet psalmist of Israel." The historical books of the Bible speak of David's considerable accomplishments as a musician, singer, and composer of poems. King Solomon followed in the footsteps of his father by writing some Psalms (72 and 127), while the authors of many of the uncredited psalms are believed to have been contemporaries of David whom he placed in charge of Jerusalem's worship.

Organization

There are several ways to understand the organization of the 150 psalms. One way is to see that Psalms is made up of five books, perhaps an imitation of the five books of Moses called the "Pentateuch"

(Genesis, Exodus, Leviticus, Numbers, and Deuteronomy). The five books within Psalms are:

Book 1: Psalms 1 to 41
Book 2: Psalms 42 to 72
Book 3: Psalms 73 to 89
Book 4: Psalms 90 to 106
Book 5: Psalms 107 to 150

Each book concludes with a doxology, or praise to God, usually found within the last verses of each of the five books. Psalm 150 serves as a concluding doxology to book 5 as well as to the entirety of Psalms.

Categories

While there are a number of different ways to categorize the psalms, there are seven general categories into which we can classify the 150 psalms.

Hymns of praise were used by individuals and by the community to offer praise to God for who he is and for his greatness and his beneficence toward the whole earth. Hymns of praise begin with a call to worship and offer reasons for praise.

Laments constitute the largest group of psalms, and these include individual and corporate laments and penitential laments. On the emotional spectrum, laments are the polar opposite of hymns of praise, openly expressing distress with deep, honest fervor. Laments usually include a complaint, a curse on enemies, and either a confession of sin or protest of innocence, and most resolve with praise to God and determination to trust him.

Thanksgiving psalms were used in circumstances opposite from those of laments or were offered in response to an answered lament. They gave individuals or groups the words to express their gratitude to God.

Salvation history or *remembrance* psalms review the history of God's saving works among the people of Israel, especially his deliverance of them from bondage in Egypt and his establishment of them as a people.

Royal or *kingship* psalms focus on the human king of Israel and the city of Zion in which he reigns, while others proclaim God as king.

Wisdom psalms praise the merits of wisdom and the person who lives a wise life. They emphasize the contrast in consequences between living a life of wisdom and a life of wicked rejection of God and his ways.

Songs of trust provide God's people with words for expressing their trust in God regardless of circumstance.

Why are these categories or genres important for us to understand as we study the psalms? Because they guide us to read the text rightly. For example, wisdom psalms must be read as Wisdom Literature, which means that we read its statements as general principles and not as promises. Laments must be read as human emotion and not as propositional truth. In royal psalms we need to think through whether it is the divine king or a human king being referenced and consider the implications of the psalm through the lens of God's everlasting intentions to reign over his covenant people.

3. Read each of the psalms below and determine which of the seven categories you think each psalm fits into: praise, lament, thanksgiving, salvation history, royal, wisdom, or trust.

1. Psalm 13 _____
2. Psalm 21 _____
3. Psalm 23 _____
4. Psalm 100 _____
5. Psalm 112 _____
6. Psalm 136 _____
7. Psalm 138 _____

It is true that the psalmists express a lot of distressing emotions throughout the 150 psalms. In fact, about sixty-seven of the 150 could be categorized in part or as a whole as lament psalms—psalms that complain to God about the psalmist's circumstances and cry out to God to act. Virtually all of the lament psalms include the following elements, though perhaps not in this order:

~ *Introductory cry or addressing of God.* The psalmist identifies the one to whom the psalm is prayed, the one he is turning to for help, the Lord. Example: "Give ear to my words, O LORD" (Ps. 5:1).

~ *Complaint.* The psalmist pours out what the trouble is and why the Lord's help is being sought. Example: "In arrogance the wicked hotly pursue the poor" (Ps. 10:2).

~ *Trust.* The psalmist immediately expresses trust in God. Example: "But I have trusted in your steadfast love; my heart shall rejoice in your salvation" (Ps. 13:5).

~ *Request for deliverance/reason for God to act.* The psalmist calls on God to act and offers reasons he should do so. Example: "Turn, O LORD, deliver my life; save me for the sake of your steadfast love" (Ps. 6:4).

~ *Assurance.* The psalmist expresses the assurance that God will deliver. Example: "O LORD, you hear the desire of the afflicted; you will strengthen their heart; you will incline your ear" (Ps. 10:17).

~ *Praise.* The psalmist realizes what God can and will do for him, which leads him to offer praise. Example: "I will sing to the LORD because he has dealt bountifully with me" (Ps. 13:6).

4. Many psalms may have a historical connection, and it is believed that David wrote Psalm 3 when he was fleeing from Absalom (2 Samuel 15–18). To develop skill in identifying the common elements of lament psalms, read Psalm 3 and note which of the six elements of a lament psalm described above is being expressed in the verses indicated.

O LORD, how many are my foes!   _____
    Many are rising against me;
many are saying of my soul,
    there is no salvation for him in God. *Selah*   _____
But you, O LORD, are a shield about me,
    my glory, and the lifter of my head.
I cried aloud to the LORD,
    and he answered me from his holy hill. *Selah*
I lay down and slept;
    I woke again, for the LORD sustained me.

> I will not be afraid of many thousands of people
>> who have set themselves against me all around.   _____
> Arise, O LORD!
>> Save me, O my God!   _____
> For you strike all my enemies on the cheek;
>> you break the teeth of the wicked.   _____
> Salvation belongs to the LORD;
>> your blessing be on your people! *Selah*   _____

5. The psalms of lament are a model of godly response to suffering. Rather than expecting us to remain stoic through our suffering, God wants us to pour out our hearts and souls to him. He also, however, wants us to remember his loving care for us and how he has forgiven our sins. This will help us trust him in the future. What are your prayers for help like in times of trouble? And what do you learn from the elements of lament psalms that should shape your prayers?

6. As we begin to think about how we can see Jesus in the Psalms, read through Psalm 3 again, recognizing that Jesus is the Lord we call out to, Jesus is our brother who understands the difficulties of living in this world, and Jesus is our deliverer. What difference does it make in how you understand this psalm and how you experience it, when you think of singing this song to Jesus?

Teaching Chapter

I Can't Stop This Feelin'

If you're like me, when you hear certain songs, it takes you back to a particular time in your life when that song was playing on the radio or on your record player. This one takes me back to 1974 when I was in junior high:

> *Ouga Chaka, Ougua Ouga, Ouga Chaka, Ouga Ouga.*
> I can't stop this feelin' deep inside of me.
> Girl, you just don't realize what you do to me.
> When you hold me in your arms so tight.
> You let me know everything's all right.
> I-I-I I'm hooked on a feelin'
> I'm high on believin'
> that you're in love with me.[2]

And this one was popular a year later, in 1975:

> Feelings, wo-o-o feelings,
> Wo-o-o, feel you again in my arms.[3]

This is one of those songs that at first you couldn't get enough of, and then it seemed like it would never go away.

Love or hate these songs, I bet you knew the words to them. And why is that? How is it that we can't remember the name of someone we met five minutes ago or have known for years, but we can call up all the lyrics to some silly song from our childhood?

There was a reason we learned our ABCs not by saying them but by singing them. Songs we sing become impressed upon our memories, don't they? In fact, some of the songs we learn as children are still in our hearts and on our lips at the very end of our lives. Most of us know of people who, in their final days on this earth, when they could not recognize their own children or put together a sentence, could sing all of the words to a favorite hymn. "Rock of Ages, cleft for me. Let me hide myself in Thee."

It makes you think about the kind of songs you want to learn while you still have all of your mental faculties, doesn't it? If the songs we sing become implanted in our souls and psyches so that they flow out of us when we no longer have control over our speech and song, don't we want those songs to be full of wisdom, full of calling out to the God who saves us, full of praise to the God who rules over all things?

This is exactly why God has given us the Psalms. While up to this point in the Bible the dominant voice has been that of God speaking to his people, in Psalms it is the human voice we hear responding to God.[4] And through this inspired discourse in the Psalms, God is also speaking to us, instructing us on how to pray and praise. The Psalms direct our outcries of distress as well as our outbursts of praise. They show us how to look at our problems through the lens of the larger reality of God's covenant commitment to us, and as we do, our problems come into proper perspective.

All of us have voices inside our heads that tell us how to think, what to do, and how to feel. And sometimes, we think, "I can't stop this feeling deep inside of me." But is that true?

Many people would say that you feel what you feel and that feelings are outside of morality or even spirituality—that they are neither right nor wrong, neither spiritual nor unspiritual; they just *are.* And many people are quick to point out that the psalmists seem to have great freedom to vent their honest feelings. And certainly we need their example of honesty and desperation before God. But are they merely venting? Or is something far more significant happening here that instructs us in what to do with our doubts and fears and desperation? Is there something here that can help us when we think we just can't stop the feelings raging inside?

No one sings about honest feelings like the psalmists do. These are songs we want to know the words to. These are songs we want to have impressed upon our minds, believing that they will shape and instruct our feelings, because in the Psalms the negative always leads to the positive. Doubt leads to trust; anger toward God turns to admiration for God; sadness gives way to joy.[5]

The psalms serve as an invitation to pour out our honest emotions before God. But they also show us that God intends to change how we feel. We expect God to give us instruction about what we should *do* and to present us with doctrine we are to *believe*, but some of us have never considered that God presents us with feelings to *feel*. As God renews our minds through the power of his Word, he changes the way we *think*. And when we *think* differently and *believe* differently, we begin to *feel* differently because our emotions flow out of what we really believe is true in the deepest parts of ourselves (not just what we think we ought to believe).

This is why we sing the songs of the Bible's hymnbook—so its wisdom will permeate us and become a part of us. We want the psalms to shape not only our thoughts about God but our feelings about him and life in this world he has made. The psalms provide us with a vocabulary for expressing the broad range of human emotions—even, or perhaps especially, the negative ones—to God in a way that draws us toward him rather than estranging us from him. They coach us in worship that is both pleasing to him and beneficial to us, which includes expressing both our gladness and our sadness.

"Let the Word of Christ Dwell in You Richly": Singing Psalms

Paul says to "let the word of Christ dwell in you richly, teaching and admonishing one another in all wisdom, singing psalms and hymns and spiritual songs, with thankfulness in your hearts to God" (Col. 3:16). Let the word of Christ go deep; let it permeate your thoughts and emotions; let it dwell in you and well up in you not in a small or reserved way but richly. And how does the word of Christ dwell in you richly? As you sing psalms, hymns, and spiritual songs. Paul's encouragement is to let the Psalms become such a part of you that when life puts the squeeze on you, this word of Christ implanted in you by the Psalms will flow out of your life and off of your lips.

But wait a minute, we want to say. How are the Old Testament Psalms the "word of Christ"? If we want to read about Christ, we usually go to the Gospels and the rest of the New Testament. In what way does the "word of Christ" specifically dwell in us richly when we read or sing psalms?

> *The psalms serve as an invitation to pour out our honest emotions before God. But they also show us that God intends to change how we feel.*

Many of Jesus's disciples were good little Jewish boys who grew up singing the psalms. They knew that some of the psalms spoke of the promised Messiah. Yet there was something they could see only in shadows as they sang these songs as children—something that became clearer when Christ came. After Jesus's resurrection when he spent forty days with them, opening up their minds to understand the Old Testament—shining the light of Christ on it—their understanding of the Psalms and the rest of the Old Testament opened up. It is this understanding we need if we want to understand how the word of Christ can dwell in us richly as we read and sing the Psalms.

We read in Luke 24 that on the road to Emmaus, as Jesus walked with two disciples, "beginning with Moses and all the Prophets, he interpreted to them in all the Scriptures the things concerning himself" (v. 27). Then, a short time later, he appeared to the rest of his disciples and said, "These are my words that I spoke to you while I was still with you, that everything written about me in the Law of Moses and the Prophets and the Psalms must be fulfilled." Luke continues writing, "Then he opened their minds to understand the Scriptures" (vv. 44–45).

Jesus worked his way through the Law of Moses and the writings of the prophets and the Psalms, helping the disciples to see that it was all about him—who he would be and what he would do to accomplish the salvation of sinners. He helped them to understand that while much of what they read about in the Psalms was accomplished in his first coming, other aspects of his work will come to fruition in his second coming.

Jesus grew up as a Jewish boy also, listening to the Law and Prophets being read and singing the Psalms. While there is so much we don't know about Jesus's boyhood, Luke tells us that Jesus "increased in wisdom" (Luke 2:52). In a way that is far too mysterious for us to grasp, the fully human Jesus grew in his understanding of his identity as the Promised One.[6] As he read the Old Testament and as he sang its psalms, he grew in his understanding of the rich tapestry of its people and patterns, its story, symbol, and song. And "where others saw only a fragmented collection of various figures and hopes, Jesus saw his own face."[7] He heard the timbre of his own voice.

Hearing the Voice of Jesus in the Psalms

Where might Jesus have seen his own reflection and heard his own voice when he read the Psalms? The reality is that he saw it on every page. But let's just look briefly at a couple of obvious places. The writer of Hebrews puts these words of Psalm 22 in Jesus's mouth:

> I will tell of your name to my brothers;
>> in the midst of the congregation I will sing your praise.
> (Heb. 2:12; cf. Ps. 22:22)

Later, the writer of Hebrews says it is Jesus speaking in the words of Psalm 40:

> Consequently, when Christ came into the world, he said,
>
> "Sacrifices and offerings you have not desired,
>> but a body have you prepared for me;
> in burnt offerings and sin offerings
>> you have taken no pleasure.
> Then I said, 'Behold, I have come to do your will, O God,
>> as it is written of me in the scroll of the book.'"
> (Heb. 10:5–7; cf. Ps. 40:6–8)

We know that psalms were on Jesus's lips at the lowest time of his life. It was the words of Psalm 22:1, "My God, my God, why have you forsaken me?" that he cried out in agony from the cross (Matt. 27:45). In fact, his final words on the cross were those of Psalm 31:5: "Father, into your hands I commit my spirit!" (Luke 23:46).

So, Jesus, who felt with us the pain of life in this world and who put his faith in God's promises in the midst of that pain, sings the Psalms with us. But Jesus is also the one about whom the Psalms are sung. Jesus repeatedly pointed to himself as the suffering servant and sovereign king that the Psalms spoke about:

- When the children were crying out to him in the temple, "Hosanna to the Son of David!," Jesus said, "Have you never read, 'Out of the mouth of infants and nursing babies you have prepared praise?'" (Matt. 21:15–16; cf. Ps. 8:2). Jesus was claiming to be the Lord worthy of the praise of infants of Psalm 8.
- After telling the parable of the tenants who killed the vineyard owner's son, which obviously spoke of the Jewish rejection and determination to kill Jesus, he said, "Have you never read in the Scriptures: 'The stone that the builders rejected has become the cornerstone'?" (Matt. 21:42; cf. Ps. 118:22). Jesus was claiming to be the rejected stone of Psalm 118.
- When the Pharisees gathered together asking whose son Jesus was, Jesus asked, "How is it then that David, in the Spirit, calls him Lord saying, 'The Lord said to my Lord, Sit at my right hand, until I put your enemies under your feet'?" (Matt. 22:43–44; cf. Ps. 110:1). Jesus was claiming to be the Lord of heaven and earth, who sits at the right hand of God until all of his enemies are under his feet, the Lord of Psalm 110.

Throughout the Gospels and into the rest of the New Testament, we see that the writers took to heart what Jesus taught them about the Old Testament, as they repeatedly emphasize how Jesus is the fulfillment of the Old Testament, including the Psalms.

So we see that Jesus sings the Psalms with us and that we sing about him in the Psalms. What difference does it make if we read the Psalms in this way? Let's look at two psalms to explore the difference it makes when the word of Christ in the Psalms begins to dwell in us richly—two psalms that most likely were originally one psalm. They are like one song with three verses and a repeated chorus. And as we hear the psalmist cry to God in Psalms 42 and 43, we will discover how God uses the psalms to change our feelings as they speak to us of Christ.

Christ's Thirst

As we read through these two psalms, we see that the psalmist moves back and forth between being overwhelmingly depressed and being ruggedly hopeful. He is a real person, and real people often take two steps forward and three steps back. He has a great desire for God but senses a great distance has come between himself and God.

> As a deer pants for flowing streams,
> so pants my soul for you, O God.
> My soul thirsts for God,
> for the living God. (Ps. 42:1–2)

The psalmist uses vivid imagery from his surroundings that helps us understand what he feels like on the inside. The first image he uses is that of a panting deer that dips his head into what should be a flowing stream only to find a dry creek bed. He feels dried up on the inside, full of longing with no relief.

We know that Jesus was fully human and felt all the human emotions we feel. Hebrews says that Jesus was "made like his brothers in every respect so that he might become a merciful and faithful high priest in the service of God, to make propitiation for the sins of the people. For because he himself suffered when tempted, he is able to help those who are being tempted" (Heb. 2:17–18). Do you think Jesus knows what it's like to feel this kind of dryness?

On the cross, we hear Jesus crying out, "I thirst" (John 19:28). Certainly Christ was physically thirsty as he hung in the hot sun. And yet when we look closely at the Gospel accounts, we realize that Jesus made no other complaints of physical pain through his time of crucifixion. Surely Jesus was speaking of a far deeper and more desperate thirst than what he felt physically. On the cross Jesus experienced the unquenchable dryness and thirst that you and I deserve to feel forever because of the distance our sin has put between us and a holy God. And yet, because Christ experienced this dryness and distance from God in our place, we can drink forever from springs of living water and never be thirsty again. When we see how this psalm points us to Christ, we remember that Christ has bridged the gap between us and God so that we can draw near.

Have you experienced what it is like to be close to God only to find yourself far away from him? That's the experience the psalmist is describing. He finds himself homesick for God, longing to feel close to him again, asking:

> When shall I come and appear before God? (Ps. 42:2)

The difficulties of life seem to mock his dependence on God so that he says:

> My tears have been my food
>   day and night,
> while they say to me all the day long,
>   "Where is your God?" (Ps. 42:3)

How does a believer fight back against all of these discouraging thoughts and oppressive emotions? He challenges them rather than giving in to them. He confronts them rather than letting them defeat him. You are not crazy to talk to yourself; you are wise to do so. The psalmist pours out his complaint to God, but he also intentionally remembers and recites how good it was to be close to God, and so he speaks to his own soul:

> Why are you cast down, O my soul,
>   and why are you in turmoil within me?
> Hope in God; for I shall again praise him,
>   my salvation and my God. (Ps. 42:5–6)

Rather than listening to his own desperate thoughts, he speaks the truth to those thoughts. Rather than trusting his feelings, he defies them.

Rather than talking about the truth of the gospel as something out there for other people, he applies it to himself personally. He prays to God, and he preaches hope to himself in the midst of his desperate dryness and despair.

And notice what he longs for most. It is not simply relief from his problems, whatever they may be. "I shall again praise him, my salvation and my God," he says. He longs to become a glad worshiper of God once again. He wants abundant praise to fall from his lips rather than angry complaints.

Christ's Struggle for Breath

In the first part of the psalm the psalmist uses the hot, dry desert of southern Israel to describe how he feels. And later he takes us to another place that provides a metaphor for the ache in his soul. He takes us just north of the Promised Land, outside of its borders, to where the streams and waterfalls flowing down from Mount Hebron create the headwaters of the Jordan River:

> Deep calls to deep
> > at the roar of your waterfalls;
> All your breakers and your waves
> > have gone over me. (Ps. 42:7)

The psalmist feels dryness like that of deer who cannot find water, and he also feels as though he's drowning. Do you know what it is like to feel like you are drowning in difficulty, like you can hardly keep your head above water?

Surely Jesus also experienced the sense of suffocation of one who is drowning, as he struggled for breath when he hung upon the cross and spiritually as he felt the weight of our sin pressing down on him. When we see Christ in this psalm, we are able to feel fellowship with him as one who understands what it is to be overwhelmed and under so much pressure that you struggle for breath.

> By day the LORD commands his steadfast love,
> > and at night his song is with me,

a prayer to the God of my life. (Ps. 42:8)

Here, in the center of the psalm, it is as if the psalmist finds his footing as he reminds himself of the steadfast love of God even as the waves of God's sovereign plans for his life wash over him. He finds his footing in the truth that the Lord's love does not come and go like the waves but is steadfast in the midst of the waves. Even though it is very dark, he hears the love song of God being sung into his ear, reminding him that his feelings of drowning in his difficult circumstances are not what define his reality but that God's covenant love is his security in the storm. And once again the psalmist shakes himself back to the truth and tells himself what to do:

> Why are you cast down, O my soul,
>> and why are you in turmoil within me?
> Hope in God; for I shall again praise him,
>> my salvation and my God. (Ps. 42:11)

I can almost picture him standing in front of the mirror telling himself: "Hope in God!" He's a little bit like the character Al Franken used to play on *Saturday Night Live* who would look at himself in the mirror and say, "I'm good enough and I'm smart enough and people like me!" Except the psalmist is not trying to build up his self-confidence but his God-confidence.

Christ's Deliverance

A third time the psalmist laments his circumstances, that he is being lied about and mistreated:

> Vindicate me, O God, and defend my cause
>> against an ungodly people,
> from the deceitful and unjust man
>> deliver me!
> For you are the God in whom I take refuge;
>> why have you rejected me?
> Why do I go about mourning
>> because of the oppression of the enemy? (Ps. 43:1–2)

Once again we know that Jesus knows how this feels. He was lied about and treated unjustly by ungodly people. And rather than defend his cause, he stayed silent; rather than call on God to rescue him, he absorbed all of the abuse mankind inflicted on him. Jesus showed us how to endure unjust treatment: he put his trust and hope in God (1 Pet. 2:23). On the cross Jesus put his hope in the power of God, by which he would rise from the dead, and in the plan of God, through which he would bring salvation to the people of God. His hope was not that God would deliver him *from* the mistreatment but that he would deliver him *through* it. And the same is true for us. While he may not rescue us from our difficulty, we can be certain that he will preserve us through it.

Ultimately, the fact that God has allowed this mistreatment causes the psalmist to feel rejected by God. But he knows his feelings are not telling him the truth, so he asks God to break through his emotions so he can embrace the truth:

> Send out your light and your truth;
>   let them lead me;
> let them bring me to your holy hill
>   and to your dwelling!
> Then I will go to the altar of God,
>   to God my exceeding joy,
> and I will praise you with the lyre,
>   O God, my God. (Ps. 43:3–4)

There in the darkness of his desperate thoughts and feelings, he needs the light of God's truth to dispel the darkness and light his path so he can run in God's direction. He doesn't just want to escape *from* his difficulties; he wants to escape *to* God. He wants to go to the altar of God. And on this side of the cross we know with more clarity where that altar is. It's not in a temple built with stones. We have an altar to go to before God (Heb. 13:10). Our altar is the crucified and risen Jesus. The psalmist wants a light to lead him. He could not have told us who this Christ is, or when he would come, or how he would penetrate the darkness. But on this side of the cross, we know. We have seen this light.

In times of distress we can give in to endless introspection and self-pity and stay right where we are—dry, drowning, needing deliverance. Or we can bring our distress before God and let him flood our lives with living water. We can remember that he is the rock beneath our feet; we can let his Word light our path so we can run in his direction. Our lives do not have to be defined by what we feel—as real as those feelings may be. Rather, our lives are to be defined by his redeeming love shown to us in Jesus Christ.

These two psalms and so many others teach us to talk back to our desperate God-doubting and God-diminishing thoughts. Don't allow yourself only to listen to yourself. Talk to yourself.

- When you feel afraid and forgotten, speak the Psalms to yourself: "For the LORD will not forsake his people" (Ps. 94:14). And remember that Jesus was forsaken so that you will never have to be.
- When you feel alone in your grief, talk to yourself, saying, "The LORD is near to the brokenhearted and saves the crushed in spirit" (Ps. 34:18). And remember that Jesus was overwhelmed with sorrow to the point of death.
- When you feel angry toward God, instead of making demands or accusations, talk back to yourself, questioning your assumptions about God's role and responsibility, his goodness and justice, his promises and purposes. Rehearse all that God has promised to provide for you in Christ and repent of your demands to experience all of his promises and protections in the here and now. Preach the gospel to yourself and let your anger give way to rest.
- When you feel jealous, instead of nurturing your thoughts of resentment because God has not given you what he has given to someone else, begin to recount all that God has given to you in Christ, which you do not deserve, and discover that gratitude begins to blossom where jealousy threatened to control you.

When you're wheeled into the operating room, as you stand at the grave or take the stand in the courtroom, in the depths of your loneliness as well as in the heights of achievement, let the words of the

Psalms assure you of his loving presence. You won't just know he is with you because you've read about it. You will know it because the words of the Psalms have become a part of you, shaping your view of God and his provision for you in Jesus Christ and ultimately changing how you feel.

The Psalms are the songs we want to be implanting in our heads and in our hearts now so that they will flow out of us later today when the phone rings with bad news, tomorrow, when we are tempted to find our satisfaction somewhere far away from God, and in the last days of our lives when we prepare to walk through the valley of the shadow of death. These are the songs we need, to speak the truth to our faithless feelings.

"Let the word of Christ dwell in you richly, singing psalms," recognizing that Jesus is your brother who sings *with* you as you sing. And Jesus is the Lord you sing about:

> The LORD is my shepherd; I shall not want. (Ps. 23:1)

> I lift up my eyes to the hills.
>   From where does my help come?
> My help comes from the LORD,
>   who made heaven and earth. (Ps. 121:1–2)

> One thing have I asked of the LORD,
>   that will I seek after:
> that I may dwell in the house of the LORD
>   all the days of my life,
> to gaze upon the beauty of the LORD
>   and to inquire in his temple. (Ps. 27:4)

And when you sing these songs to the Lord, you can put a human face on this Lord. Jesus is the good shepherd. Jesus is the source of your most needed help. It is his beauty we will gaze upon throughout eternity.

Looking Forward: The Song of the Redeemed

God gave psalms to his people to sing to him, to express their deepest emotions, greatest needs, and cherished hopes. Many of the psalms are the songs of a broken heart, sung by those living in a broken world. They are songs filled with aching and longing for the Lord to show up in difficult circumstances and deliver.

These are still the songs we sing. We still long for the Lord to deliver us from the difficulties of life in this world. And one day he will. When he does, he will give us a new song to sing. We will no longer need the inspired laments of the Psalms to pour out the aches in our hearts to God. We will no longer wonder out loud when he will come to save us.

We find a hymnbook for the new songs we will sing in the book of Revelation. These are the songs that will give us the words we will need, to pour out our hearts to our God. In that day our hearts will be full of overflowing gratitude, exuberant joy, and unending praise, and nothing will keep us from singing.

In John's revelation of Jesus and the celebration to come, a mighty chorus of redeemed people sing a new song we have never sung before, and yet everyone knows the words and sings along with confidence and joy! The song is new because it is no longer about Israel's deliverance from Egypt, or the coming of Messiah. The new song is about his rightful claim to rule the world.

> Worthy are you to take the scroll
> > and to open its seals,
> for you were slain, and by your blood you ransomed people for God
> > from every tribe and language and people and nation,
> and you have made them a kingdom and priests to our God,
> > and they shall reign on the earth. (Rev. 5:9–10)

This song that God gives to us does not celebrate the feelings that come with our fallenness or our concerns about the wicked who appear to be winning. This song celebrates the Lamb who was slain. This song is worthy of getting stuck in our heads and in our hearts. This is a song we want to sing along with, a song we want to know the words to, a song we long to sing one day in perfect harmony around the throne. But it won't be just redeemed people who will sing this song. The angels will join in along with us:

> Then I looked, and I heard around the throne and the living creatures and the elders the voice of many angels, numbering myriads of myriads and thousands of thousands, saying with a loud voice, "Worthy is the Lamb who was slain, to receive power and wealth and wisdom and might and honor and glory and blessing!" (Rev. 5:11–12)

Because Jesus is all-powerful in conquering death, because he is the heir of all things, and because he is all-wise and stronger than all of the forces of hell, he is worthy of all the honor, glory, and blessing that the hosts of heaven can sing to him. Revelation tells us the celebration will become even grander still, reaching its crescendo:

> And I heard every creature in heaven and on earth and under the earth and in the sea, and all that is in them, saying, "To him who sits on the throne and to the Lamb be blessing and honor and glory and might forever and ever!" (Rev. 5:13)

Our hearts will be full and we will be unable to stay silent. Every*thing* and every*one* will sing out, giving the triune God the praise and glory he deserves.

Discussion Guide

Psalms: The Songs of Jesus

Getting the Discussion Going

1. When you think of the Psalms, is there a particular psalm or phrase from a psalm that comes to your mind? Has there been an experience in your life in which a particular psalm has been especially meaningful to you?

Getting to the Heart of It

2. Many of us have a cerebral relationship with God. We like to think through the Bible's teaching and chew on its meaty truths and doctrines. But while the book of Psalms is filled with instruction and precepts, its truths are not meant to be absorbed only with the mind but must be experienced in the heart, felt with the emotions, and sung from the soul. Why do you think it is important to God that we relate to him on an emotional level?

3. What do you think it means that God wants not only to change how we think and what we do but also to change how we feel? Are there ways you think God's sanctifying work in you has changed how you feel?

4. The Pharisees asked Jesus which is the greatest commandment, and Jesus told them, "You shall love the Lord your God with all your heart

and with all your soul and with all your mind" (Matt. 22:37). How can the Psalms help us to love the Lord in this way?

5. Of course, we know that only one person truly loved the Lord with *all* of his heart, soul, and mind. Why is this important for us to remember?

6. Let's take a familiar psalm, Psalm 23, and think through how it impacts our understanding of the Psalms once we know that Jesus fulfills the Psalms as both the perfect Israelite who could pray the Psalms and the Lord of the Psalms to whom we pray. As a group, work your way quickly through various phrases of Psalm 23. How and when in his life could Jesus have prayed this psalm to his Father?

7. Now, read through Psalm 23 substituting "Jesus" for "LORD" and remembering that Jesus said, "I am the good shepherd" (John 10:11, 14). How does this add to the meaning of this psalm?

Getting Personal

8. Genuine and earnest prayer proceeds first from a sense of our need and next from faith in the promises of God. After working through the Personal Bible Study questions about the various kinds of psalms and the various elements of lament psalms, is there an aspect of prayer that you realize is weak or missing in your prayer life?

Getting How It Fits Into the Big Picture

9. Throughout this study we are considering how the particular book we are studying fits into the larger story of God's plan of redemption and his written revelation. How might our understanding of God's covenant care of his people be different if the Psalms were not in the Bible?

Blessing and Perishing in the Psalms

Blessing and Perishing in the Psalms

Psalm 1, which serves as an introduction to the entire book of Psalms, presents us with one of the primary themes not only of the Psalms but of all the Wisdom Books, and, in fact, of the entire Bible: the reality of and contrast between two groups of people and two ways of life in this world—the righteous who have embraced God's covenant from the heart and the wicked who reject God's offer of grace.

The first word of the book of Psalms, *blessed*, is actually challenging to define. *Ashrey* is the Hebrew word in Psalm 1 that is translated "blessed" in all of the places in the Bible where we read statements such as, "Blessed is he who . . ." Finding an English word to translate *ashrey* isn't easy. "Truly happy" might be the best English translation. But *happiness*, at least the way we think about happiness today, is also inadequate, as *ashrey* conveys a deep sense of well-being, contentedness, and fulfillment. This is the kind of life we all long for. While *happiness* in modern use depends upon events or happenings, *blessedness* in biblical use is not influenced by events but is based on the joy found in one's good relationship with God. The book of Psalms offers wisdom on how to experience blessedness in the kingdom of God.

1. The Bible doesn't give us a definition of *blessedness*. Instead, it repeatedly describes what the person who enjoys this blessedness is like. Blessedness is woven throughout the fabric of the Psalms, appearing

125 times. Following are just a few statements about this blessedness—one from each of the five books of Psalms. What does each of these "Blessed is" statements in the Psalms add to your understanding of blessedness?

~ Book 1: Psalm 40:4

~ Book 2: Psalm 65:4

~ Book 3: Psalm 84:4–5

~ Book 4: Psalm 106:3

~ Book 5: Psalm 146:5

2. While the biblical writers want us to know and enjoy the blessedness of God, they also present the opposite reality: those who are not blessed are actually wicked. Just as blessedness is woven through the Psalms, so is the way of the wicked. Read the following verses, again one from each of the five books in the Psalms. What insight do each of these verses provide into wickedness?

~ Book 1: Psalm 10:4

~ Book 2: Psalm 50:16

~ Book 3: Psalm 75:8

~ Book 4: Psalm 94:1–7

~ Book 5: Psalm 119:155

3. Read Psalm 1. What is the primary influence in the life of the blessed man of Psalm 1, and what does he refuse to let influence him?

4. What are the results of the blessed man's delight in and meditation on the Bible?

5. How are the wicked contrasted with the blessed in Psalm 1 in each of the following categories?

Significance: The wicked are like _____. (v. 4)

The blessed are like _____. (v. 3)

Stability: The wicked are _____. (v. 4)

The blessed are _____. (v. 3)

Standing: The wicked _____. (v. 5)

The blessed _____. (v. 6)

Salvation: The wicked _____. (v. 6)

The blessed _____. (v. 3)

6. Notice that "the LORD knows the way of the righteous" (v. 6). What do you think are some things the Lord knows about the way of the righteous? Do you find this comforting or threatening?

7. We are told that while the blessed man *prospers*, the way of the wicked will *perish*. How would you define what these two words mean in this psalm, recognizing that they are intended by the psalmist to be opposite from each other?

The psalmist says about the blessed man, "In all that he does, he prospers" (v. 3). Yet we know that many of the psalms actually lament that the opposite appears to be true. Many of the psalms lament that the wicked are prospering while the righteous are suffering. How do we make sense of this seeming incongruity? We must understand what kind of literature we are reading when we read wisdom literature in the Bible.

Wisdom psalms do not offer blanket guarantees but rather make observations on general patterns of life. When readers fail to take the literary genre of the wisdom psalm or proverb into account and read a statement from Wisdom Literature and "claim it" as a promise, they misunderstand the intent of the text, and this misunderstanding and misappropriation often lead to disappointment and even disillusionment with God. We must remember that the psalms are poetry, and what may appear to be a specific promise is often the psalmist drawing a picture for us in material terms we can grasp of the spiritual blessedness of belonging to God.

While the psalms don't promise that only good things will happen all the time to the Lord's people, they do affirm that those who put their hope in the Lord are indeed blessed. They are blessed because they have relationship with the Lord who is himself the blessing of the righteous. The righteous enjoy the inherent blessing that comes from following God's law and avoiding paths of sin that often result in pain and misery.

Often the blessing for those who trust in the Lord does include special measures of physical or material blessing. The psalms express a spiritual optimism based on the recognition that God is a faithful, righteous, and loving father. So it is never wrong, as a child of God, to ask your Father for the favor and blessing that only he can provide. But as we do so, we remember, "My flesh and my heart may fail, but God is the strength of my heart and my portion forever" (Ps. 73:26).[1]

8. When we read "Blessed is the man" in Psalm 1, it reminds us of the teaching of Jesus that we find in the New Testament, especially in the Sermon on the Mount. The blessedness of the beatitudes is the covenantal happiness of Psalm 1. Similar to Psalm 1, the Sermon on the Mount begins with "Blessed" and ends with the perishing of the man who rejects God's word. Once again, two opposite realities are woven into the sermon and span the sermon beginning to end.

Psalm 1:6 says, "The LORD knows the way of the righteous," and the Beatitudes found in Matthew 5:3–12 could be summarized as the "way of the righteous." The opposite of the Beatitudes is to walk in the counsel of the wicked. To help you to really think through these familiar statements, read through the Beatitudes on the next page and compose their "opposite" in keeping with the sample provided.

Blessed are the poor in spirit, for theirs is the kingdom of heaven. (Matt. 5:3)	*Perishing are those who arrogantly think they are "in" with God because of their own perceived goodness, for they will never enjoy God's rule over their lives.*
Blessed are those who mourn, for they shall be comforted. (Matt. 5:4)	
Blessed are the meek, for they shall inherit the earth. (Matt. 5:5)	
Blessed are those who hunger and thirst for righteousness, for they shall be satisfied. (Matt. 5:6)	
Blessed are the merciful, for they shall receive mercy. (Matt. 5:7)	
Blessed are the pure in heart, for they shall see God. (Matt. 5:8)	
Blessed are the peacemakers, for they shall be called sons of God. (Matt. 5:9)	
Blessed are those who are persecuted for righteousness' sake, for theirs is the kingdom of heaven. (Matt. 5:10)	

Teaching Chapter

Secure in the Storm

David and I were preparing to get on a plane to fly to Bogotá, Colombia, for twelve days of ministry around the South American country, and we knew we needed prayer. So after a Sunday morning service, we went to two elders in our church and asked them to pray for God to do something significant through us as we headed into something for which we felt very inadequate. We told them where we were going and what we would be doing, after which one of the elders looked at us and said, "Are you sure about this? Do you know how dangerous Colombia is?"

The next Sunday we were in Villavicencio, Colombia, a city on the edge of Colombia's jungles, where we put our arms around people whose husbands and sons had been kidnapped by guerrillas only to be returned dead or never heard from again. These are people who live day to day in the shadows of great danger.

That night, when we got back to our hotel room, we turned on the television and saw reports of unprecedented flooding in Nashville. And when we got online, one of the Nashville television stations was streaming live a shot from helicopters flying over our neighborhood, much of which was under water. We couldn't help but think that we were safer there in our hotel room in the "dangerous" country of Colombia than we would have been in the "safety" of our own home.

We think we know how to ensure our security. But do we? We

certainly go to great lengths in pursuit of it. We take vitamins, buy insurance policies, wear our seatbelts, and install alarm systems, all in an attempt to create security. But can we, in a world that is repeatedly rocked by volatile stock markets, deadly viruses, natural disasters, and random violence, ever be truly secure?

What is real security, and is it possible to have? Psalm 1, which, along with Psalm 2, serves as an introduction to the entire Psalter, helps us to find an answer to this question. This psalm defines two ways of life—one that leads to ultimate security and the other that leads to ultimate insecurity.

Blessed Is the Man

The first word of the first psalm is "Blessed." "Blessed" as it is used in Psalm 1 isn't a word we use in modern English, so we have to seek to understand what it meant in the ancient world of the psalmist. Sometimes the best way to understand something is to define it by its opposite.

If I sneeze, "Ah-h-h-h-choo!" what do you do? You say, "Bless you." Why?

There was a day in the premodern world when sneezing was a symptom of the plague. And getting the plague was considered a sign of God's displeasure. So, saying, "God bless you," when someone sneezed was offering a prayer that the person would receive the blessing of God—ongoing life—rather than perish under God's displeasure.

They understood something that we find in the very first psalm and throughout the Psalms—that blessing is the opposite of perishing. While the first word of Psalm 1 is "Blessed," the last word of the psalm is "perish." The poet placed these words at opposite ends of the psalm to illustrate to us that they are opposite in meaning. Blessedness and perishing are opposite realities.

The Bible doesn't really give a definition of *blessed*, but it does show us what defines one who is blessed. We have "blessed is the man who," and "blessed is everyone who," and "blessed is the nation whose " over twenty times in just the Psalms.

What the Blessed Man Rejects

The first thing we learn in Psalm 1 about what defines the person who enjoys so much blessedness is what he rejects.

> Blessed is the man
> > who walks not in the counsel of the wicked,
> nor stands in the way of sinners,
> > nor sits in the seat of scoffers. (Ps. 1:1)

He does not walk, or stand, or sit. These words seem to describe a progression of engagement that makes its way through "thinking, behaving, and belonging."[2] He doesn't absorb the ideas and values or follow the advice of those who live their lives assuming that God is irrelevant. He doesn't conform to the behavior or lifestyle of those who sin with no conscience. He doesn't keep company with cynics who get a good laugh by making fun of the things of God.

It's not that this person isn't tempted by the materialism and hedonism and cynacism of those around him. It's not that he has put his head into the sand and retreated from engaging with the culture. This is a person who refuses to let that culture shape how he thinks, what he does, and what he enjoys. Does this describe you? Are you the "man" of Psalm 1?

- Are you the single woman who finds herself alone because you refuse to enter into the hook-up culture that is considered to be enjoying a healthy sex life?
- Are you the one on the outs with the office crowd because you don't laugh at the crude sexual humor everybody else finds so funny?
- Are you the mom or dad who is willing to be unpopular with the team and/or the coach because you put the worship of God with God's family before the game that is scheduled for when your church family gathers to worship?
- Are you the high-school or college student who will not sit on your couch and watch that terribly funny comedian who mocks not only religion (which oftentimes deserves to be mocked) but also the Christ you love and the truths you hold dear?

Let's face it. The "blessed man" is someone who just doesn't fit in. He doesn't go where everybody else is going, and he doesn't run with the "in" crowd; he doesn't laugh along with the latest raunchy viral video. Frankly, it is easier and oftentimes a lot more fun to conform rather than to chart a course that goes against the grain. But if we don't have the strength to refuse to conform, we will never find the happiness Psalm 1 talks about or enjoy the security it offers.

What the Blessed Man Enjoys

It's not that this person cannot be influenced by anything. It is that the central driving, shaping influence in his life is not the advice offered on afternoon television or the philosophy of the latest best-seller or what his neighbors will think. It is something quite different.

> But his delight is in the law of the LORD,
>   and on his law he meditates day and night. (Ps. 1:2)

Either we are shaped by the ungodly world around us, or we are formed and shaped and remade by the Word of God.

What is the "law of the LORD"? It's simply the teaching of the Bible. This man implants the Word of God in his mind and soul. He doesn't drag out his Bible every now and then because he knows he ought to. He finds it fascinating, thrilling, and invigorating. Rather than looking forward to chewing the fat with those who have no interest in God or what God has to say to them, he looks forward to chewing on the rest of the chapter he started reading this morning and finishing the word study he started last week. More important than watching her favorite TV show is spending time with her Bible open. The Scriptures are the controlling influence in this person's life.

We're getting the idea from the psalmist that there are not a number of lifestyles to pick and choose from but really only two ways. Either we are shaped by the ungodly world around us, or we are formed and shaped and remade by the Word of God.

What the Blessed Man Expects

So the person who enjoys this blessedness is defined by what he rejects and what he enjoys. Then the psalmist continues helping us to understand and desire this blessedness by describing what this person expects, using contrasting similes.

> He is like a tree
>> planted by streams of water
> that yields its fruit in its season,
>> and its leaf does not wither. (Ps. 1:3)

This is not a tree that just happened to sprout up any ol' place. It has been expertly placed by the one who planted it in suitable soil by streams of water where its roots can go deep and draw the nourishment it needs to be fruitful. It produces what it is meant to produce. The sun beats down on it, and the harsh winds blow against it, and it does not wither away.

In a word, this man is secure. He's not easily blown off course but is durable and fruitful. The Word at work in his life is producing what it is meant to produce—love, joy, peace, patience, kindness, goodness, gentleness, faithfulness, and self-control (Gal. 5:22). It's not that he never expects to face difficulty; it's that when he does, his roots are so deep in God that he is not shaken.

The psalmist then shifts away from the simile of the tree and says outright:

> In all that he does, he prospers. (Ps. 1:3)

What does the psalmist mean here? What kind of prosperity is he talking about? Does this mean that if you delight in the Word of God and meditate enough, your business will make a big profit, and you'll have the family you always dreamed of, and you won't have car accidents or get cancer? It might. Those who walk according to God's law avoid paths of sin that often result in pain and misery. They walk on paths of truth, righteousness, and goodness, which have inherent blessing in them. While these kinds of blessings are not the constant experience of the faithful believer, the psalmist is a spiritual optimist, knowing that he has a loving Father who delights in giving good gifts to his children (see Luke 11:13).

But by "prosper," the psalmist is saying that the Word of God that you delight in and meditate on will have its intended effect. It will make a profound difference in the outcome of your life. The Word of God will be successful in what it set out to do, which is to so firmly ground you that nothing can ultimately harm you.

What the Wicked Should Expect

The description of what the wicked should expect couldn't be more different:

> The wicked are not so,
>   but are like chaff that the wind drives away. (Ps. 1:4)

Whereas the blessed man was like a tree that is strong, secure, rooted, fruitful, and evergreen, the wicked are "like chaff that the wind drives away." *Chaff* is the husks around a grain of wheat or barley. The ancient practice was to beat the grains of wheat to separate the husks and then to toss the threshed wheat high into the air so that the wind would blow away the husks while the heavier wheat grain gathered on the ground. The chaff was worthless, lightweight, and disposable, and it simply blew away in the wind.

Using this simile, the psalmist sets before us descriptions of two kinds of people living life in two dramatically different ways. One is secure and successful, invulnerable to whatever winds might blow. The other is insecure and unsubstantial, vulnerable to being carried away by the wind into nothingness.

The psalmist is painting a picture of a stark difference between these two kinds of people, these two ways of life, isn't he? And we know people who love the Bible, people who are substantial and whose lives are fruitful. But do you know any wicked people? It seems a little harsh, doesn't it? It seems to us that there must be some middle ground to stand on.

We come to this psalm assuming that the "righteous" are good people and the "wicked" are bad people. But even with that we're uncomfortable with the rigidness of those categories. We look around at other people and at ourselves and say, "Well, I'm not perfect, but I'm certainly not wicked!"

Who are "the wicked"? We know plenty of people who are not interested in God, but we wouldn't necessarily say that they are "wicked." In fact, we know plenty of really good people who do lots of good things—they are kind and generous and caring. Does the fact that they have no interest in the one true God, no interest or perhaps only a passing interest in the truths of the Bible, really mean that they are what the Bible would call "wicked"?

We don't easily absorb this perspective, but it is clearly the perspective of the Scriptures. Let's look at it from another angle. Think about Jesus's answer to the question, "What is the greatest commandment?" He said, "You shall love the Lord your God with all your heart and with all your soul and with all your mind" (Matt. 22:37). If this is the greatest good, would it not make sense that the greatest evil is to refuse or neglect to love the Lord your God with all your heart, soul, and mind?

Being kind to others and a good citizen of the world or even religiously sincere doesn't make up for rejecting the one who made you and has chosen to reveal himself to you through his Word. Being an incredibly nice or generous person does not make up for having no interest in God. The Bible's word for this way of life, this kind of person, is "wicked."

> *Are you willing to fully embrace the Bible's perspective on what is good and what is evil, what lasts and what fades away, what is secure and what is vulnerable, and who is blessed and who is wicked?*

At some point we have to decide if we are going to absorb the wisdom, the value system, and the way of looking at the world and ourselves that is presented to us in the Bible, rejecting our culture's dominant viewpoint, or if we are going to go with the flow, go with what makes sense to the pundits and opinion shapers of this world, and perhaps even to ourselves. Are you willing to fully embrace the Bible's perspective on what is good and what is evil, what lasts and what fades away, what is secure and what is vulnerable, and who is blessed and who is wicked?

The psalmist has given us a definition and a description of bless-edness and wickedness using images and similes, and he leaves us speaking more directly about what the wicked and the righteous can anticipate in the future—the true test of security or vulnerability:

> Therefore the wicked will not stand in the judgment,
>   nor sinners in the congregation of the righteous;
> for the LORD knows the way of the righteous,
>   but the way of the wicked will perish. (Ps. 1:5–6)

The psalmist fast-forwards to the future—to the day when all will stand before God in the judgment. What are seemingly good people going to say when they stand before the God in whom they have had no inter-est? According to this psalm, they will have nothing to say and no leg to stand on. They "will not stand." It will not matter how large their checks to charity have been, or how small their carbon footprint has been, or how many good deeds they have done. No amount of saving, giving, or doing will add up to any real security under the withering judgment of God. Big insurance policies and savings accounts will offer no security in this economy. The way of the wicked, the way of those who live life with no reference to the one true God but only for themselves according to their own ideas, doing things their own way, and assuming they can provide their own security, will perish.

Who Is "the Man" of Psalm 1?

Who did the writer of this psalm have in mind when he wrote about this man whose delight is in the law of the Lord and who meditates on it day and night? Does anyone really do this? We know that many of the psalms were written about Israel's king, and many of those are specifi-cally about David. Is he "the man who delights himself in the law of the Lord" of Psalm 1? Let's take a step back to get a wider view of the Bible's search for this man.[3]

If we go back to Deuteronomy, we find a description of what the king of Israel was to be when the day came that Israel demanded a king:

> When he sits on the throne of his kingdom, he shall write for himself in
> a book a copy of this law, approved by the Levitical priests. And it shall be

> with him, and he shall read in it all the days of his life, that he may learn
> to fear the LORD his God by keeping all the words of this law and these
> statutes, and doing them. (Deut. 17:18–19)

This sounds like the man whose delight is in the law of the Lord, who meditates on it day and night, doesn't it? Perhaps when Israel has a king, the king will be this man.

Later, before the time of the kings came, we see that God required something similar of Joshua, the leader of God's people:

> Only be strong and very courageous, being careful to do according to all
> the law that Moses my servant commanded you. Do not turn from it to the
> right hand or to the left, that you may have good success wherever you
> go. This Book of the Law shall not depart from your mouth, but you shall
> meditate on it day and night, so that you may be careful to do according to
> all that is written in it. For then you will make your way prosperous, and
> then you will have good success. (Josh. 1:7–8)

It sounds as if Joshua is to be the man of Psalm 1; certainly he prospered in all that he did. Then came David, the great king who reigned over Israel and wrote:

> The law of the LORD is perfect,
>   reviving the soul;
> the testimony of the LORD is sure,
>   making wise the simple;
> the precepts of the LORD are right,
>   rejoicing the heart. . . .
> Moreover, by them is your servant warned;
>   in keeping them there is great reward. (Ps. 19:7–8, 11)

Certainly this sounds like the Psalm 1 man.

In 1 Kings 2 we overhear David on his deathbed, telling his son Solomon how he is to live:

> I am about to go the way of all the earth. Be strong, and show yourself a
> man, and keep the charge of the LORD your God, walking in his ways and
> keeping his statutes, his commandments, his rules, and his testimonies,
> as it is written in the Law of Moses, that you may prosper in all that you do
> and wherever you turn. (1 Kings 2:2–3)

Wasn't David telling Solomon to be the man of Psalm 1?

We expect the leader, the king of God's people, to be the man of Psalm 1. With such a leader, the people could perhaps be the "congregation of the righteous" that the psalmist refers to in verse 5. But we know what happened in Israel's history. No leader, no king—not David and certainly not Solomon or any of his successors—turned out to be the man of Psalm 1. Far from meditating on it day and night, the people of Israel actually lost the Book of the Law. It was unearthed in the days of king Josiah, and when he had the book read, the disaster of what had happened became clear:

> When the king heard the words of the Book of the Law, he tore his clothes. And the king commanded Hilkiah the priest . . . "Go, inquire of the LORD for me, and for the people, and for all Judah, concerning the words of this book that has been found. For great is the wrath of the LORD that is kindled against us, because our fathers have not obeyed the words of this book, to do according to all that is written concerning us." (2 Kings 22:11–13)

Rather than being the congregation of the righteous, the nation of Israel had become the wicked. They didn't delight in the law of the Lord but instead walked in the counsel of the wicked and stood in the way of sinners and sat in the seat of mockers. And the Old Testament recounts how judgment came, a judgment in which they did not stand but fell and were blown away like chaff into exile.

When the book of Psalms was compiled, in the years following their return from exile, all the people who read it would have been well aware of this history and their inability to find or to be the man of Psalm 1. The people of Jesus's day were also aware of this history, though they still loved to think of themselves as righteous rather than wicked. When they read Psalm 1, they saw themselves as "the man," as "the congregation of the righteous." They thought they were secure in their adherence to religious law, when, in truth, they were vulnerable to judgment. Jesus did not mince words with the religious leaders of his day but instead warned them of the judgment they would face, saying, "You also outwardly appear righteous to others, but within you are full of hypocrisy and lawlessness" (Matt. 23:28).

Jesus came to those who thought they were "the man," those who thought they were in the "congregation of the righteous," helping them to see that, in fact, they were desperately and hopelessly wicked apart from him. He came to offer himself to all who would confess their own wickedness and turn to him to be their righteousness.

> For Christ also suffered once for sins, the righteous for the unrighteous, that he might bring us to God. (1 Pet. 3:18)

Jesus is the only truly righteous one. He was "the man" of Psalm 1 as no leader or king in Israel ever managed to be. Jesus delighted in the law of the Lord (Heb. 10:7, quoting Ps. 40:8). He prayed day and night (Luke 5:16; 6:12; 9:18, 28; 11:1; 22:39–40). He meditated so profoundly on Scripture that he quoted it in the most extreme moments of his life.[4] He was like a tree, abundantly fruitful, and all he did prospered. His life, death, and resurrection accomplished just what was intended—the salvation of sinners, the salvation of people like you and me who can never live up to the demands of Psalm 1. "For God so loved the world, that he gave his only Son, that whoever believes in him *should not perish* but have eternal life" (John 3:16).

What Do We Do with Psalm 1?

The intended message of Psalm 1 is not that you must try really hard to avoid the wrong crowd and try really hard to love your Bible. What would be the real security in that? How far away from the way of the wicked would you need to walk, and what if you missed a day or a night or a week or a month or a year meditating on the law of the Lord? Can any man or woman really live like this man the psalmist describes? Can anybody really be this consistent, this persevering, and this pure?

The truth is, you and I simply cannot delight in the law of the Lord apart from Christ. "Without him, the law is nothing but a curse to us, a witness against us."[5] Only because Jesus obeyed the law perfectly in our place can we delight in the law of the Lord rather than despair. Only because he endured the judgment we deserve can we expect to stand in the judgment, not because of our own righteousness but because of his.

When we look at Psalm 1 in the light of Christ, we realize that this psalm is not just about two ways of living intended to get us to try harder to live the right way and feel guilty for our inability to live that way. It is about Jesus and his people. He did not walk in the counsel of the wicked or stand in the way of sinners or sit in the seat of mockers. And neither will you as you are united to him and draw your life from his. His delight is in the law of the Lord, and yours will be too as his Spirit lives inside you giving you new appetites and desires for God's Word. He is like a tree planted by streams of water and is so strong and secure that even death could not destroy him. And if you are joined to him, neither can death destroy you. This is the security we need. In fact, this is the only true security there is.

> *Only because Jesus obeyed the law perfectly in our place can we delight in the law of the Lord rather than despair.*

Grace enables you to be the person of Psalm 1 who does not take the advice of the wicked or scoff at the Word of God like the wicked do. This grace goes to work in your life transforming your aversion to the Bible and boredom with the Bible into a love for the Bible that goes to work in you, making you durable enough to withstand the storms of life. This foundational truth of Psalm 1 was echoed by Jesus in the Sermon on the Mount:

> Everyone then who hears these words of mine and does them will be like a wise man who built his house on the rock. And the rain fell, and the floods came, and the winds blew and beat on that house, but it did not fall, because it had been founded on the rock. And everyone who hears these words of mine and does not do them will be like a foolish man who built his house on the sand. And the rain fell, and the floods came, and the winds blew and beat against that house, and it fell, and great was the fall of it. (Matt. 7:24–27)

Notice that there is much about the wise man and the foolish man that is the same. They both hear the teaching of the Scripture. It is like they are both sitting in church Sunday to Sunday. The second similarity is that they both experience the storm. The same harsh winds of difficulty blew through both of their lives.

But there is a key difference between these two men. Did you catch it? When the wise man hears the words, he "does them" whereas when the foolish man hears the words he "does not do them." Another version says the wise man "puts them into practice" (NIV), and a Bible paraphrase says that you are like this smart carpenter if you "work these words into your life" (MESSAGE). This is certainly the same wise man we saw in Psalm 1, isn't it? This is a man who delights in the law of the Lord and meditates on it day and night.

When the storm comes to the man who has not only heard but also worked the Word of God into his life, his house does not fall. His life is built on a solid foundation. He is secure. But when the storm blows into the life of the man who heard the Word but ignored it or rejected it, his house collapses. Everything about his life falls apart. He has no solid foundation for facing the storms of life. No security. His life is a picture of perishing.

I began by telling you about our trip to Bogotá and the flood that took place in Nashville while we were there. On that Sunday night when David and I were in Bogotá, we were able to get a text from our next-door neighbor letting us know that the floodwaters that overtook many of our neighbors' homes did not submerge the homes in our cul-de-sac. And we were grateful. But David and I do know what it is like to feel the cold winds of difficulty and loss blow into our lives. We have buried two of our three children and have felt waves of sorrow roll over us, threatening to crush us. In the years since, we've often had people ask us: "How did you survive that? How did your marriage survive it? And how is it that you have joy?" And the only way I know to answer is to tell them that years before the storm of suffering blew through my life, God began building a solid foundation in my life to stand on as I left behind my casual, nonessential approach to the Bible and began reading, studying, responding to, and being changed by God's Word. I worked his words into my life so that when the storm came, though I was not unaffected by it, neither was I destroyed by it.

I suppose many people would look at our family and suggest that

God did not come through on the psalmist's promise to prosper us. Others might assume, like Job's friends assumed, that we are not among the righteous if something so hard would happen in our lives. But I think they're wrong. The Word of God had its intended effect in our lives. It gave us stability in the storm and a security that extends beyond the bounds of this life, a future of infinite security into which we have relinquished two of our children. Some people might say we've had incredibly bad luck. We would say that we are blessed.

Real security is not found in trying really hard to be the man of Psalm 1. It is found only in being united to the only man who was able to live this way, the one who was truly and perfectly righteous. United to him, his Word becomes our daily food, our delight day and night. When we are joined to him by faith, we can rest easy in peaceful security. We need not fear that the winds of difficulty that blow in our lives will destroy us. We can be sure that God's Word at work in our lives will have its intended effect. It will prosper. It will make us strong, like a tree—a tree that will stand tall and green and fruitful no matter what storms may come.

Looking Forward: The Wicked Will Not Stand

In Psalm 1, we've been looking at two ways to live and their very different outcomes. We've seen that the way of the righteous leads to life while the way of the wicked leads to death. Certainly the godly experience this abundant happiness in life in the here and now in many ways. To live life walking away from evil and in the way of the Lord means that we avoid many of the miseries that are the natural consequences of a life lived with no reference to God. And certainly the wicked experience the diminished life this psalm suggests in the here and now as they move through their days with no orientation to Christ, no resource outside of themselves for love or joy or peace that the righteous have in the Holy Spirit. But in Psalm 1 the psalmist is looking farther ahead, from this life into the life to come, when he writes that "the wicked will not stand in the judgment" (Ps. 1:5). The psalmist looks beyond this life to the day when every person will stand before God to give an account of his or her life. This is the same scene John describes in Revelation:

> Then I saw a great white throne and him who was seated on it. From his presence earth and sky fled away, and no place was found for them. And I saw the dead, great and small, standing before the throne, and books were opened. Then another book was opened, which is the book of life. And the dead were judged by what was written in the books, according to what they had done. (Rev. 20:11–12)

Notice that when we stand before this judgment seat, there will be the "books" and there will be "the book of life." The key to understanding how we will be judged on that day is understanding the difference between the "books" and "the book of life."[6]

What's written in the "books" is all that you've done and all that you've failed to do. For those who are hoping to get into heaven on the basis of their good deeds, hoping that their good deeds outweigh their bad deeds, the books will offer only condemnation. As Paul said, "None is righteous, no, not one" (Rom. 3:10). No one is saved by the record of his or her deeds. But while what is written in the "books" spells *condemnation* for those who are depending on their own goodness, what is written there will serve as *confirmation* for those who are connected to Christ in a saving, transforming way. The books will show how you threw yourself on his mercy and welcomed his forgiveness, how your appetites and affections changed as his Holy Spirit was at work in you. The books provide an accounting of all the things God's grace in your life has empowered you to do and become because of your connectedness to Jesus.

The "book of life" is quite different from the "books." It is a record of the names of all those God calls his own. These are the blessed of Psalm 1, those whom God "has blessed . . . in Christ with every spiritual blessing in the heavenly places, even as he chose [them] in him before the foundation of the world, that [they] should be holy and blameless before him" (Eph. 1:3–4).

John continues in Revelation:

> And if anyone's name was not found written in the book of life,
> he was thrown into the lake of fire. (Rev. 20:15)

Here again we see the scene described in Psalm 1 that tells us "the way of the wicked will perish" (Ps. 1:6). This is ultimate eternal perishing. This is the very sad reality in the midst of the abundant happiness of the righteous of Psalm 1, the end to which the wicked will come because of their rejection of Christ. They will perish.

Is there really any sadder word, any sadder reality, in the whole Bible, than "will perish"?

Blessing and Perishing in the Psalms

Getting the Discussion Going

1. Do you think most people today think that there are good people and bad people? What would they say is the difference?

Getting to the Heart of It

2. The Wisdom Books replace our human wisdom with godly wisdom. After studying Psalm 1 this week, how would you define and describe who is righteous and who is wicked?

3. What is the difference between someone who walks in the counsel of the wicked, stands in the way of sinners, and sits in the seat of scoffers, and someone who is salt and light in the midst of a corrupt world?

4. What is the difference between someone who delights in the law of the Lord and someone who does her daily duty of having devotions?

5. Psalm 1 makes clear that everyone is either in a state of blessing or perishing. How can a person know which state he or she is in?

6. It is the wisdom of Psalm 1—that God blesses the righteous and punishes the wicked—that Job's friends embraced. How does understanding many of the statements of the Wisdom Literature as observations

on general patterns of life rather than as blanket guarantees help us with this tension?

7. How does an understanding of God's justice in the life to come (which the Old Testament saints did not have in the fullness that we do, because of further revelation we've been given in the New Testament) help us with our frustrations when we see the good suffer and the wicked succeed?

8. Those who read Psalm 1 in Old Testament times had less light when they read it than we have. How do we read and understand it differently because we read it through the lens of the finished work of Christ?

Getting Personal

9. The psalmist calls us to the blessedness of delighting in and meditating on God's Word day and night. Some of us struggle with that. Let's talk for a moment very practically about what this means. What practices or habits have helped you to do this? What has hindered you in developing an affection for God's Word and a habit of consistent meditation on it?

Getting How It Fits into the Big Picture

10. Throughout this study we are considering how the particular book we are studying fits into the larger story of God's plan of redemption and his written revelation. In what way does the blessing of life given to the righteous, who embrace God's covenant from the heart, and the perishing of the wicked, who refuse God's gracious offer of mercy, describe the whole storyline of the Bible?

The Royal Psalms

Personal Bible Study

The Royal Psalms

It is a common misunderstanding that the idea of the kingdom of God was something introduced by Jesus. Certainly there was a freshness and an urgency about his announcement that "the kingdom of God is at hand" (Mark 1:15). But Jesus was not putting a totally new concept before a bewildered audience. His Jewish listeners knew very well that God is king. Their Scriptures stated it often enough, and they sang words to that effect regularly from the Psalms in their synagogue worship. As we study the kingship or royal psalms today, we have the benefit of being able to read these psalms through the perspective of the ultimate king who came. So as we look at several royal psalms, we'll be looking for the ways in which Christ fulfilled what was written in the Psalms about that king in his first coming and the ways in which he will fulfill them when he comes again to reign forever on the renewed earth.

Before we look at a handful of specific royal psalms, it would be helpful to take a step back to see the structure of the Psalms as a whole. Perhaps you've never seen any structure to the Psalms but have seen the book as a randomly assembled collection of all different kinds of psalms with different tones and perspectives. But there is a shape to the Psalms, a sense of a storyline to its five books that is closely related to the theme of kingship. A simple overview of the aspects of the story presented in each of the five books of Psalms could look like this:

> Book 1: Psalms 1 to 41: God established his king in the world.
> Book 2: Psalms 42 to 72: The world rebelled against God as king.
> Book 3: Psalms 73 to 89: Even God's king rebelled against God as king.
> Book 4: Psalms 90 to 106: But God is still king.
> Book 5: Psalms 107 to 150: God's king will come.

While many of the psalms were written by Israel's King David during the time of his reign, the book of Psalms was actually collected into its current form much later, at a time when there was no king on the throne in Israel. The sad reality of Israel's history is that after several centuries, the Davidic kingdom became corrupt. Just two generations after David was installed on the throne, the kingdom split into a northern and a southern kingdom with David's line ruling only over the southern king-dom. Two and a half more centuries went by with kings coming and going in all kinds of cruelty, abuse of power, and idolatry. Eventually the leaders of the northern kingdom were carted off into captivity under the Assyrian Empire. Another century and a half went by, and, despite occasional times of revival and renewal, the southern kingdom fell to the Babylonians who carried them off into exile.

In time, some of the people came back. They began to rebuild the temple that had been burned down, but the new one never compared to the great temple built by Solomon, and there was no king reigning on Israel's throne. It was during this time that the Psalter was compiled into its current form. So the Psalms were a helpful reminder of the past faithfulness of God's promises to David and his line as well as a source of hope that God would, indeed, fulfill all of the promises he made regarding a king to sit on David's throne forever.

Sprinkled in each of the five books of Psalms are royal psalms related to the activities of the king, such as coronation (Psalms 2, 110); a royal wedding (Psalm 45); issues related to war (Psalms 18, 20, 144); ruling in righteousness and justice (Psalms 72, 101); and the promises related to the Davidic covenant (Psalms 89, 132). Remembering that Jesus said that everything written about him in the Psalms must be fulfilled (Luke 24:44), we realize that all of the royal psalms speak not only of David and his descendants but of David's ultimate descendant who sits on David's throne.[1]

Psalm 2 is a psalm David wrote for his own coronation, which was likely used at the coronation of future kings in the Davidic line. This psalm is one of the most quoted or alluded to in the New Testament. Consider how the following New Testament passages help us to see that while this psalm was originally about David, ultimately it is about the greater David, Jesus. Read Psalm 2 and then answer the questions below.

1. According to Acts 4:24–28, who do the "kings of the earth" who "gathered together against the Lord and against his Anointed" in Psalm 2 ultimately refer to?

2. According to Acts 13:32–34, who is the "Son" in Psalm 2?

3. According to Romans 1:4, what event established Jesus's royal sonship as described in Psalm 2 (as opposed to his divine sonship, which is from eternity past)?

4. What aspect of Psalm 2 do you see described in Revelation 2:27 that will be fulfilled at the return of Christ?

5. What aspect of Psalm 2 do you see described in Revelation 6:16–17 that will be fulfilled at the return of Christ?

6. What aspect of Psalm 2 do you see described in Revelation 19:15 that will be fulfilled at the return of Christ?

Read Psalm 45. This psalm was likely written for a particular historical royal wedding of a Davidic king, perhaps Solomon. But difficulty comes in verses 6 and 7, where the king, who is a man, seems to be addressed as God (Elohim):

> Your throne, O God, is forever and ever.
>> The scepter of your kingdom is a scepter of uprightness;
>> you have loved righteousness and hated wickedness.
> Therefore God, your God, has anointed you
>> with the oil of gladness beyond your companions. (Ps. 45:6–7)

7. According to Hebrews 1:6–7, who does the writer of Hebrews indicate this psalm is speaking about?

8. In what ways do you see a fulfillment of Psalm 45, especially verse 3 and 4, at the end of time as described in Revelation 19:6–16?

Psalm 72 is a prayer asking that God would bring about his rule on the earth through the reign of the king on David's throne. It is likely that this psalm was composed by David for Solomon. As a father, he is praying that the reign of his son will reflect the justice of God and the blessings that flow forth from such a righteous reign. While some aspects of this prayer were answered by God in Solomon's reign, it is also apparent that the psalm is not ultimately fulfilled in Solomon. Christ is the fulfillment of the hopes and prayers of Psalm 72, as in him the petitions become reality. But they must be understood in light of both his first and second comings.

9. How do the following passages reveal how God answers the prayers of Psalm 72 in Christ?

Give the king your justice, O God, and your righteousness to the royal son! (Ps. 72:1)	John 5:30; Rom. 3:24–26
May he defend the cause of the poor of the people. (Ps. 72:4)	Matt. 11:5

May he have dominion from sea to sea, and from the River to the ends of the earth! (Ps. 72:8)	Matt. 28:18–20
In his days may the righteous flourish, and peace abound, till the moon be no more! (Ps. 72:7) May all kings fall down before him, all nations serve him! (Ps. 72:11) May the whole earth be filled with his glory! (Ps. 72:19)	Rev. 21:22–27

Psalm 110 deals with the role of the house of David in the life of God's people, but like other royal psalms, it goes well beyond the achievements of any merely human heir of David and thus looks forward to the Messiah. The central theme of Psalm 110 is the Messiah's warfare against the enemies of God.

10. In Matthew 22:41–46 and Mark 12:35–37 we find an account of Jesus quoting Psalm 110:1. What is he trying to communicate through his question about this psalm?

11. The idea that the risen and ascended Jesus is seated at God's right hand until his enemies are his footstool, in fulfillment of Psalm 110:1, is presented in numerous places throughout the New Testament. What do you think this kingly image intends to communicate about the person and work of Jesus?

12. Psalm 110 is unique in that while we find that the offices of priest and king in the Old Testament point to Christ, this is one of the few places where we find that the Messiah will uniquely be both priest and king. Hebrews 5:5–10 brings Christ's royal sonship and royal priesthood together. What does the writer of Hebrews want us to know about Jesus as priest from these verses?

Teaching Chapter

Royal Wedding

Did you scoop up some memorabilia to commemorate the decade's most significant social event? You know what I'm referring to, don't you? I'm talking about the royal wedding of Prince William to Kate Middleton. There were plenty of interesting things to collect in order to remember it forever. I'm not talking mugs or magnets or tea towels or coins or spoons. There were much better things than that.

You could have purchased a life-size cardboard cutout of the happy couple to have them as guests at your next party. Castle Rock Brewery brewed a special ale called "Kiss Me Kate." But the ultimate piece of memorabilia—and forgive my making fun if you bought one of these for your home—is the royal refrigerator. The distributor for GE appliances in the UK offered a side-by-side refrigerator freezer emblazoned with one of the official engagement photographs of the couple. Imagine—you could have had William and Kate cuddling in your kitchen for years to come.

Now, if none of these things appeal to you, in fact, if you thought you would throw up if you had to endure one more gushy media story about Kate's dress or the royal honeymoon, or wonder how soon there will be a baby royal, what you really should have purchased was the Royal Wedding Sick Bag. This paper bag was marketed to "those who can't stomach a big, expensive wedding celebration."

Maybe you got sick of the media's slobbering coverage. But admit it: you were at least a little bit interested, weren't you? Something in us has a fascination with royalty. My theory is that we can thrill at the pageantry and pomp of the British royals only because they have no real authority, certainly no authority over us who long ago threw off British rule. They're benign. Somehow we don't have the same attitude about royalty in other parts of the world. As we witness people in a number of countries in northern Africa and the Middle East risking their lives to relieve themselves of long-term dictators who intended to transfer power to their own sons, effectively ruling the countries as dynasties, we realize that we are not intrigued or enamored by *all* royalty. When we think about most kings who have ruled over history, we get less excited about the ways of royals, because the truth is, when humans have unchecked authority, that power is most often abused. No one can genuinely celebrate life under a corrupt or cruel king.

But what if we could live under a good king, a king who is not corrupt but compassionate, a king who does not enslave but serves, a king who does not take the lives of those he reigns over but gave his life to save those who are citizens of his kingdom?

The Bible is the story of this good king and his kingdom. We were made to live under the gracious rule of this king. Genesis begins with the creation of the kingdom of God in the garden of Eden, where Adam and Eve lived in willing obedience to God's word and rule. But then a rival regime established a beachhead in God's kingdom. And the rest of the Bible is the story of God's restoration of a people to be the willing subjects of his perfect rule, living with him in his kingdom on a restored earth.

When God promised Abraham that his descendants would possess the Promised Land and be the people of God under his authority, he was describing his kingdom. When he rescued Israel out of captivity in Egypt, it was so that he could bring them into the place where the kingdom would be established. And when his people demanded a human king like those of all of the peoples around them, he accommodated their request, giving them a king who was to be his vice regent, ruling his people at his behest.

When God set David on his royal throne over Israel, he made a covenant promise to him—that his throne would last forever and that one of his descendants would eventually rule the whole world. But to understand Psalms rightly, we are going to have to figure out how to deal with the tension between the utterly remarkable promises made to David and the historical reality that a few generations later there was no king on David's throne.

Last week we studied Psalm 1, which, with Psalm 2, serves as an introduction to the entire book of Psalms. And while we looked last week at the blessed man who delights in the Lord, this week we will look at the royal king who reigns over the world. We will discover that ultimately they are one and the same person. Understanding Psalm 2 will help us to understand the rest of the royal psalms in the psalter and even the storyline of the psalter and, in fact, the storyline of the entire Bible.

Psalm 2 was likely composed to be read or sung at David's coronation and the coronation of all the kings in the Davidic line to follow after him. It is like a script for four speakers to use at this royal event. As we read it and seek to "hear" it this way, we identify the four speakers in the psalm: first, the Lord's enemies; second, the Lord himself; third, the Lord's Anointed; and finally, the Lord's ambassador, the psalmist.[2]

The Lord's Enemies Speak

> Why do the nations rage
>   and the peoples plot in vain?
> The kings of the earth set themselves,
>   and the rulers take counsel together,
>   against the LORD and against his Anointed, saying,
> "Let us burst their bonds apart
>   and cast away their cords from us." (Ps. 2:1–3)

From last week, when we studied Psalm 1, remember that the blessed man was "meditating" on God's law. The same word that was translated "meditating" there is translated "plot" here. But whereas in Psalm 1 the blessed man was giving his mental energy and best thinking to understanding and obeying God's Word, here, those who hate God are giving all of their best energy and thinking toward a quite different goal. They are not trying to figure out how to obey but rather how to overthrow God's authority.

We read this and think, *Oh, those terrible people; what are they thinking?* Those must be evil people—people on the fringe of society—who *would* think this way about God. As usual when we read the Old Testament, we immediately identify ourselves with the good guys and not the bad guys. But the uncomfortable reality is that we all conspire to overthrow the authority of God in our lives. We want to be free of any restraint; we don't want to live the way God has prescribed. We've got our own ideas about what we ought to do. We want autonomy, not authority. While we want to be free to choose God's way when it suits us, what we want most is to keep our options open. We are happy for the boundaries God has set for us to serve as general guidance, but we don't want to be enclosed by them. We don't want to obligate ourselves to strict obedience. We do not want to be ruled.

The essence of sin is rejecting the authority of God. Until the gospel takes root and blossoms in our lives, we see his rule as "bonds" and "cords." Deep in our hearts we think God's ways are a heavy burden on us that turn us into slaves, until he gives us eyes to see that it is our sin that enslaves us and only in him can we find true freedom.

But notice that this rebellion is not just against God. It is against "his Anointed." Who is this? The Hebrew word used here is *mashiach*, which in Greek is *christ* and in English is *messiah*. This is the word used in the Old Testament for priests and kings who had oil poured on them in order to set them apart for a special function.[3] Anointing with oil was symbolic of the outpouring of the Spirit of God on the king to empower him for his duties as king. This messiah or anointed one was originally David and his descendants who were set apart by God to serve as kings over his people.

So in the first stanza of Psalm 2, we see that the Lord's enemies—which is all those who do not want God to exercise authority in their lives—are making a declaration of independence from God and from the king he has put in place.

The Lord Himself Speaks

Having heard the raging voices of God's enemies running around the earth plotting together, the next voice we hear speaking in the psalm is the voice of God, who is seated in serenity, unperturbed, confident, enthroned in heaven. The psalmist wants us to grasp the absurdity of the hostility of humanity against the authority of God.

> He who sits in the heavens laughs;
>> the Lord holds them in derision.
> Then he will speak to them in his wrath,
>> and terrify them in his fury, saying,
> "As for me, I have set my King
>> on Zion, my holy hill." (Ps. 2:4–6)

The Lord of heaven is not threatened by the rebellion of earth, wondering what he is going to do to regain some semblance of control. He sits high above our petty desires for so-called freedom. Here we are, stamping our feet and waving around our little crowns, saying, "I want to be king of my own life. I want to do things my way. You are not the boss of me" (sounds like something we would laugh at if our children said it, right?). To God, our temper tantrums and attempts to dethrone him are ridiculous. In Psalm 2 we see that "first he laughs, then he scoffs, then he rebukes, and then he terrifies. First he is amused, then he is bemused, and then he becomes angry, and finally his fury is released."[4]

"I have set my King on Zion," the Lord says. It is as if he is saying that those who are plotting rebellion don't even realize that the battle is already over. He has put the king of his choosing, the king whom he installs and empowers, in the place of authority. God has put David on the throne in Zion—David and Solomon and all of the kings in their line.

But in a sense, they were only the warm-up act for the king God intended to put on this throne one day. It is if they were only keeping the seat warm for the greater king whom God intended to set on his holy hill. David and Solomon were God's messiahs with a small *m*. They were the Lord's anointed for their day. They held the office of messiah until Messiah came. They were royal sons of God in the role of king. But they were only small-s sons, preparing the way and pointing toward the Son who would come.

The New Testament opens with Matthew's presentation of the genealogical tree of Jesus, showing that Jesus was a direct heir to King David's throne. John records that when Andrew found his brother Simon, he said to him, "We have found the Messiah" (John 1:41), and he took him to Jesus.

Jesus himself repeatedly made clear that he was indeed the Messiah, the descendant of David that all of the messiahs and sons of David who had sat on David's throne were pointing toward, when he said, "The time is fulfilled, and the kingdom of God is at hand" (Mark 1:15).

Those who had eyes to see saw that Jesus had authority that could only have come from God. As he worked miracles in their midst, he proved that he had authority over demons, authority over nature, authority over sickness, authority to forgive sins, and even authority over death. When he opened his mouth to teach, there too he had authority, "for he was teaching them as one who had authority, and not as their scribes" (Matt. 7:29). As you can imagine, those scribes didn't appreciate the authority of Jesus's teaching, which diminished their own. Luke records:

> One day, as Jesus was teaching the people in the temple and preaching the gospel, the chief priests and the scribes with the elders came up and said to him, "Tell us by what authority you do these things, or who it is that gave you this authority." He answered them, "I also will ask you a question. Now tell me, was the baptism of John from heaven or from man?" (Luke 20:1–4)

Jesus's way of responding to their question was to ask them a question, a riddle of sorts. Whichever way they answered, it presented a challenge to their own authority. This back-and-forth conversation of riddle-like questions continued with the scribes asking, "Is it lawful for us to give tribute to Caesar, or not?" (Luke 20:22); and concerning the woman who had been married to seven brothers, they asked, "In the resurrection, therefore, whose wife will the woman be?" (v. 33). Rather than being trapped by their questions, Jesus transcended them with his teaching. At the end, Luke records that the scribes didn't dare ask Jesus any more questions. But Jesus wasn't done. He had one more riddle for them:

> He said to them, "How can they say that the Christ is David's son? For David himself says in the Book of Psalms,
>
>> "The Lord said to my Lord,
>> Sit at my right hand,
>>> until I make your enemies your footstool."
>
> David thus calls him Lord, so how is he his son?" (Luke 20:41–44)

There Jesus was quoting Psalm 110, a psalm the scribes and everyone else who was listening in knew well. When David wrote Psalm 110, it is as if he was recording a divine conversation that he had overheard. He heard "The Lord," meaning "Yahweh" or "Jehovah," speaking to the Davidic king. But interestingly David calls the king "my Lord," which implies that David saw this king as greater than himself. How could one of his descendants actually be greater than David himself? In Jewish categories, the father always had dominance over the son. This was the greatest riddle of all time that had no answer until the only person who could be both David's son and David's Lord stood in front of them.

The implication of Jesus's riddle-like question was clear. He was saying, "I am the one who is David's son as well as the one to whom David is subject. I am the king God has always intended to send to sit on David's throne. I am God's own son. This is where I get my authority."

God, in Psalm 110, was speaking ultimately to the Christ, his Messiah, who was Jesus. And after Jesus's resurrection and ascension, what God had said to him about sitting at his right hand was fulfilled. When Peter preached his first sermon at Pentecost, he said:

> This Jesus God raised up, and of that we all are witnesses. . . . For David did not ascend into the heavens, but he himself says,
>
>> "The Lord said to my Lord,
>> Sit at my right hand,
>>> until I make your enemies your footstool."
>
> Let all the house of Israel therefore know for certain that God has made him both Lord and Christ, this Jesus whom you crucified. (Acts 2:32–36)

Peter's argument was that Psalm 110's promise of one ascending to sit at God's right hand could not be applied to David, because David died. Therefore, Peter is arguing, it must apply to the resurrected and ascended Jesus, David's greater son.

And his conclusion is that Jesus is "both Lord and Christ." The title "Lord" would have particular meaning to Gentile ears. During the first and second centuries, citizens of Rome were required to take a loyalty oath and say publicly, *"Caesar curios,"* which means "Caesar is lord." Peter was proclaiming the royal authority of Jesus over non-Jewish people. And "Christ" had great meaning for Jewish ears. This was the office of royal kingship. To modern ears, "Christ" can sound like simply Jesus's surname, as in Jesus, son of Mr. and Mrs. Christ. But for the Jewish people who had been waiting and longing for *the* Christ, this had tremendous meaning. Peter was proclaiming Jesus to be the Christ, the anointed one of the Psalms.

> *In God's sovereignty over history and by his inspiration of Scripture, David and his kingship, and even his enemies, were always meant to point forward to Jesus and his kingship and his enemies.*

A couple of chapters later, in Acts 4, Peter once again affirmed that Jesus is the anointed one of Psalm 2 as he spoke of Jesus's enemies:

Through the mouth of our father David, your servant, said by the Holy Spirit,

> "Why did the Gentiles rage,
>   and the peoples plot in vain?
> The kings of the earth set themselves,
>   and the rulers were gathered together,
>   against the Lord and against his Anointed"—

for truly in this city there were gathered together against your holy servant Jesus, whom you anointed, both Herod and Pontius Pilate, along with the Gentiles and the peoples of Israel, to do whatever your hand and your plan had predestined to take place. (Acts 4:25–28)

So, when we read Psalm 2, we must realize that when the enemies of the anointed one speak, they are foreshadowing the enemies who will put Christ on the cross. In God's sovereignty over history and by his inspiration of Scripture, David and his kingship, and even his enemies, were always meant to point forward to Jesus and his kingship and his enemies. The writer of Hebrews said that everything in the Old Testament was "a shadow of the good things to come instead of the true form of these realities" (Heb. 10:1). The reign of David is a shadow cast backward into history by the reign of Jesus Christ.

The Lord's Anointed Speaks

And as we continue in Psalm 2, we get to hear the anointed one, who was originally David and, now we know, ultimately Jesus, speak about what God has decreed for him and for history, which opens a window into the mind of God and his secret plans.

> I will tell of the decree:
> The LORD said to me, "You are my Son;
>   today I have begotten you.
> Ask of me, and I will make the nations your heritage,
>   and the ends of the earth your possession.
> You shall break them with a rod of iron
>   and dash them in pieces like a potter's vessel." (Ps. 2:7–9)

On his coronation day, as David was installed as God's representative to reign over his people, David entered into a new and unique relationship with God, one of royal sonship. And likewise, when Jesus began his ministry, though he had been eternally the Son of God in the presence of God, he entered into a new relationship with God the Father—that of royal sonship.

No less than an audible voice from heaven affirmed that Jesus was the greater David, the true Son Psalm 2 points to. When Jesus was baptized, and later when he was transfigured, a voice from heaven said, "This is my beloved Son, with whom I am well pleased" (Matt. 3:17; 17:5). And clearly this is what the apostles understood, as Paul later preached in Antioch:

We bring you the good news that what God promised to the fathers, this he has fulfilled to us their children by raising Jesus, as also it is written in the second Psalm,

> "You are my Son,
>   today I have begotten you." (Acts 13:32–33)

Paul makes clear that the Son of Psalm 2 is Jesus. The Son, in Psalm 2, says that God told him only to ask, and he would give him the nations for his inheritance. And in the Gospel of John, we get to overhear Jesus doing just that. In his prayer immediately prior to his crucifixion Jesus prayed, "Father, the hour has come; glorify your Son that the Son may glorify you, since you have given him authority over all flesh, to give eternal life to all whom you have given him" (John 17:1–2). We, as believers, are the inheritance Jesus asked for.

The Lord's Anointed in Psalm 2 speaks of God's giving him power over his enemies. Just as David, the Lord's anointed, needed only to ask and God would grant him power over his enemies, to make them part of his own kingdom, so Jesus, the Lord's Anointed, needed only to ask God to grant him power over those who were his enemies. And in overcoming death, Jesus indeed overcame his enemies.

The Lord's Ambassador Speaks

In the final stanza, it is the psalmist who speaks; the poet becomes preacher and issues an appeal to all who will listen.

> Now therefore, O kings, be wise;
>   be warned, O rulers of the earth.
> Serve the LORD with fear,
>   and rejoice with trembling.
> Kiss the Son,
>   lest he be angry, and you perish in the way,
>   for his wrath is quickly kindled.
> Blessed are all who take refuge in him. (Ps. 2:10–12)

Here we remember that we are working our way through the Wisdom Books. And here is wisdom and warning to all who live on the earth: serve the Lord. And how do we do that? We kiss the Son.

Why should we kiss the Son? Because his angry wrath is quickly kindled. And this is interesting because throughout the Bible the Lord's anger is described as slow. We are told he is patient. However, this is not the anger of the Father but of the Son, and not in his first coming but in his second. It is as if the psalmist can, by inspiration of the Holy Spirit, see into the scene at the end of time that John describes in Revelation. The kings of the earth from Psalm 2 are there, as is the Son:

> Then the kings of the earth and the great ones and the generals and the rich and the powerful, and everyone, slave and free, hid themselves in the caves and among the rocks of the mountains, calling to the mountains and rocks, "Fall on us and hide us from the face of him who is seated on the throne, and from the wrath of the Lamb, for the great day of their wrath has come, and who can stand?" (Rev. 6:15–17)

The kings of the earth in this horrific scene are looking for a place to hide, and they cannot find one. They did not listen to the warning of the psalmist, because if they had, they would have known where to hide themselves so that they could have avoided the devastating wrath of the Lamb. They should have taken refuge in the Lamb. "Blessed are all who take refuge in him" (Ps. 2:12).

How does this make sense? How are we saved from the Lamb by taking refuge in the Lamb?

If you were ever a Saturday-afternoon *Lassie* watcher, you might have picked up an important lesson from the heroic hound. In an episode called "The Fire Watchers," the problem is not that Timmy has fallen into a well, but that a smoker has dropped a simmering cigarette butt in the middle of the forest during a dry spell that has started a fire, and Ranger Wade has fallen from his horse and is injured right in the pathway of the raging fire. How will Lassie save the day this time? There was only one way for Lassie to save Ranger Wade, and that was by starting another fire. She must, as they say, fight fire with fire. By lighting another fire and burning the fuel that would feed the approaching fire, Lassie was able to create a safe place for Ranger Wade to wait for rescue. This is what firefighters call going "into the black."

Only by taking refuge on ground that has already been burned can one find safety from a raging fire.

My friends, the only place to find safety from God's burning anger toward sin is in the place that has already been burned by his wrath. Jesus was enveloped in the fury of the wrath of God toward sin so that you will never have to endure those flames. The only refuge from the wrath of the Lamb in the last day will be in the Lamb. Here is true and eternal blessedness. "Blessed are all those who take refuge in him."

> *The only refuge from the wrath of the Lamb in the last day will be in the Lamb.*

The Lord Reigns

There we have it, Psalm 2, an introduction to the entire Psalter that reveals both the history and the future of the Lord's anointed one, ruling and reigning on his throne. It sets the stage for the big message of Psalms, which is "the Lord reigns. Your God is on his throne." When we come to Psalms 93–99, the psalmist seems to want to press the point repeatedly:

> The LORD reigns; he is robed in majesty. (Ps. 93:1)

> For the LORD is a great God,
>   and a great King above all Gods. (Ps. 95:3)

> Say among the nations, "The LORD reigns!" (Ps. 96:10)

> The LORD reigns, let the earth rejoice. (Ps. 97:1)

> The LORD reigns; let the peoples tremble! (Ps. 99:1)

My friend, the Lord reigns. He reigns over your family squabble and your children's struggle. He reigns over your health crisis and your financial predicament. He reigns over the longing you have for what has never happened in your life and the frustration you feel over the unwanted things that have happened in your life. God is still king, and he still reigns over the world he has made, and in your life.

God's king has come to us to inaugurate his kingdom on this earth, and he is coming again to establish it forever on a renewed earth. The day is coming when, as John wrote in Revelation, loud voices in heaven will say:

> The kingdom of the world has become the kingdom of our Lord and of his Christ, and he shall reign forever and ever. (Rev. 11:15)

And we will join in the singing, saying:

> We give thanks to you, Lord God Almighty,
>   who is and who was,
> for you have taken your great power
>   and begun to reign. (Rev. 11:17)

There will be no resistance to the authority of our king on that day, but only joyful welcome.

Maybe you find yourself today resisting the authority of your King. Perhaps you are a bit of a royal watcher who likes the idea of royalty but resents the reality of authority. You need to know that the Lord reigns and he is a good king. You can entrust yourself to him. He did not come to be served but to serve. He does not want to wear you down; he wants to lift you up. He has no intentions of taking advantage of you but wants to give to you all the advantages of belonging to him. He does not intend to put you to work but has done all the work necessary to bring you into his kingdom, his home.

The important question is: Are you willing to submit to his authority, to let his Word hold sway in your life? Or are you literally hell-bent on having your own way? "Whoever does not obey the Son shall not see life, but the wrath of God remains on him" (John 3:36). The evidence that you are a member of the royal family is your glad obedience to the King.

Do you find yourself muttering against God because you find his rules confining and burdensome? You must not have seen the King as he truly is. See him in the flesh and blood of Jesus Christ and respond to the royal invitation of this king, who said, "Come to me, all who labor and are heavy laden, and I will give you rest. Take my yoke upon you, and learn from me, for I am gentle and lowly in heart, and you will find rest for your souls. For my yoke is easy, and my burden is light"

(Matt. 11:28). Don't believe the world's lies or your own thoughts that tell you that to submit to your King will only cut short your fun and freedom. "If the Son sets you free, you will be free indeed" (John 8:36).

Be wise; be warned. Listen to the psalmist. Kiss the Son. This kiss is far more magnificent and far more significant than the kiss of William and Kate in Westminster Abbey or on the balcony of Buckingham Palace. This kiss matters not "till death do us part," but beyond the bounds of death, when we will never be apart again. This kiss is the kiss of the glad joining of our lives in covenant with our King and glad submission to his loving rule. This is the kiss that seals us so securely to Christ that we need never fear being burned by fires of his wrath. Instead we will spend eternity in his loving embrace.

Looking Forward: The Lord Reigns

In the ancient world, a victorious king would place his foot on the neck or back of an enemy as a symbolic act of domination. This is the prophetic image David depicts in what seems to be a Spirit-enabled overhearing of a conversation between Yahweh and the Messiah in Psalm 110:

> The LORD says to my Lord:
>   "Sit at my right hand,
> until I make your enemies your footstool." (Ps. 110:1)

God kept the first half of this divine promise when Christ ascended after his resurrection from the dead. "When the Lord Jesus had finished talking with them, he was taken up into heaven and sat down in the place of honor at God's right hand" (Mark 16:19 NLT). Jesus is David's Lord, who is seated at the right hand of God. And there he waits.

How do we know he waits? And what is he waiting for? The writer of Hebrews explained, "Our High Priest offered himself to God as a single sacrifice for sins, good for all time. Then he sat down in the place of honor at God's right hand. There he waits until his enemies are humbled and made a footstool under his feet" (Heb. 10:12–13 NLT). Jesus is waiting for the day Yahweh told him about, the day when everything he died to accomplish will come to its full fruition. Because while Christ has done everything required to defeat his enemies, and though his kingdom was inaugurated when he came to this earth the first time, that kingdom is yet to be consummated when he returns.

While he waits, all of his enemies are not yet subdued. But they will be. That is not in question. Otherwise he would not sit. He sits because the outcome is certain. There is no cause for alarm, even though sin and death still wield a great deal of power in this world.

> For he must reign until he has put all his enemies under his feet.
> The last enemy to be destroyed is death. (1 Cor. 15:25–26)

The day is coming when the enemies of Christ—those who have trampled on his Word, his ways, and his people—will themselves be trampled upon. Jesus, at rest and enthroned in divine glory, will put his foot upon the neck of all evil, and his victory will be complete. The King is going to come and put everything right in our lives and in the world, once and for all.

Babies will no longer be born only to be ignored by addicted mothers. Children will no longer suffer the betrayal of sexual abuse. Teenagers will no longer take their own lives in their bedrooms. Tyrants will no longer target an entire race for extinction. Tsunamis will no longer wipe out entire cities. Marriages will no longer end in divorce. Bodies will no longer be vulnerable to disease or aging. Our King will dominate and dispense with all the evil and suffering of this world, and we will worship him forever as our glorious ruler. We don't have to wonder if evil, death, and decay will have its way forever in this world. We need only look up to our King, poised to bring an end to all of his enemies.

> Behold, he is coming with the clouds, and every eye will see him,
> even those who pierced him, and all tribes of the earth will wail
> on account of him. Even so. Amen. (Rev. 1:7)

Discussion Guide

The Royal Psalms

Getting the Discussion Going

1. Let's think out loud together about what it would be like to live under a good king. What would he provide? How would he protect? What would make a king and his kingdom truly good?

Getting to the Heart of It

2. The Bible helps us understand the person and nature of God by revealing his names, his deeds, his character traits, and his roles such as father, judge, and shepherd. In the Psalms his role as king comes starkly into view. What do we uniquely come to understand and appreciate about God when we see that he is the king who reigns?

3. Did you notice in Psalm 2 that the "kings of the earth" take their stand against the Lord *and* against his Anointed? Clearly, to oppose God is to oppose his Anointed, and to oppose his Anointed is to oppose God. Jesus said, "Whoever hates me hates my Father also" (John 15:23). What does this mean for many people today who say they are interested in God or believe in God, but are not so sure about Jesus?

4. Sometimes we struggle when we read psalms in which the psalmist calls down terrible curses on his enemies. How does a deeper understanding of the Davidic king being God's representative in the world help us to make sense of those parts of the psalms?

5. How is asking God to accomplish the justice he has promised different from exacting revenge or nurturing vindictiveness?

6. Let's take a minute to look back at our work in the Personal Bible Study, in which we saw how God fulfilled his promises regarding the Davidic king through Christ. Looking back over your study, which connection between a royal psalm and its fulfillment in Jesus was especially interesting or meaningful to you?

7. At Pentecost, when Peter preached, "Let all the house of Israel therefore know for certain that God has made him both Lord and Christ, this Jesus whom you crucified" (Acts 2:36), Luke records that the people were "cut to the heart, and said to Peter and the rest of the apostles, 'Brothers, what shall we do?'" (v. 37). Later in Romans 10:9 Paul writes, "If you confess with your mouth that Jesus is Lord and believe in your heart that God raised him from the dead, you will be saved." In the modern evangelical church, we oftentimes focus on Jesus as savior without emphasizing his lordship, with some going so far as to say that you can receive Jesus as savior but not as lord. How do you think Peter or Paul might have responded to that suggestion?

Getting Personal

8. As we've studied the royal psalms this week, we've considered the appropriate response to the truth "the Lord reigns," which is submission to his authority. What assumptions or misperceptions about submitting to King Jesus keep us from freely submitting to him?

Getting How It Fits into the Big Picture

9. Throughout this study we are considering how the particular book we are studying fits into the larger story of God's plan of redemption and his written revelation. Why was it important to the Gospel writers to make clear that Jesus was a descendant of David?

Repentance
in the Psalms

Repentance in the Psalms

There are a number of psalms that are called penitential psalms, which provide us with words and direction for confessing sin, seeking forgiveness, asking for a fresh start, and celebrating the forgiveness of God (Psalms 6; 25; 32; 38; 51; 130; 143).

1. We'll begin by examining Psalm 51, which begins with the notation "A Psalm of David, when Nathan the prophet went to him, after he had gone in to Bathsheba." Explain briefly from memory, or from reading 2 Samuel 11:1–12:15, what incident this notation is referring to.

2. According to Psalm 51:1, what does David know about God that gave him the courage to cry out to him for forgiveness?

3. In Psalm 51:1–2 David uses three words to describe his sin. What are they, and what do they each mean? (A dictionary or Bible dictionary might be helpful.)

4. David also uses three terms or images in Psalm 51:1–2 to describe what he wants God to do in regard to his sin. What are they, and what do you think they mean?

5. In Psalm 51:3–6, what does David say that he knows about himself and about God?

∼ About himself:

∼ About God:

6. In Psalm 51:7 David asks God, "Purge me with hyssop and I will be clean." Read Exodus 12:21–23 and Hebrews 9:18–20. How does this help us understand what David is asking for?

7. In addition to the request that God purge him with hyssop, David asks God to do a number of other things in Psalm 51:8–12. Write a few sentences putting David's requests in your own words.

8. In Psalm 51:13–15 David expresses what he wants to do instead of sin. What is it?

9. How might Psalm 32 be a fulfillment of the desire David expressed in Psalm 51:13–15?

10. In Psalm 32:1–2, what does David say makes a person truly happy and deeply satisfied?

11. Using vivid imagery, David describes in Psalm 32:3–4 what it felt like before he confessed his sin. What was it like?

12. According to Psalm 32:5, what was the breakthrough for David?

13. Think back over the past week, or month, or even year. What specific sins can you remember confessing to God and asking him to wash them away from your life? (If, for privacy concerns, you do not want to write these in this book, find a piece of paper to write them on. But don't avoid this important exercise.)

14. If you have a hard time thinking of any of your specific sins, what do think is needed in your life to enjoy the blessedness that this psalm promises?

Teaching Chapter

"Wash Me"

I was going back and forth via e-mail with the South American ministry that had invited David and me to come to Colombia for twelve days, when they sent this message: "Would you be interested in sharing your testimony with a group of prostitutes?"

What else do you say to an invitation like that except yes? But what was I going to say to these women? What do I know about the broken dreams and broken promises that brought them to such a hard life?

A week later, 250 prostitutes, crowded into a small concrete room in a neighborhood feeding center in one of Bogotá's worst neighborhoods, sat looking up at me expectantly. They weren't hard like I had expected. They were hurting. And before I knew it, they handed me the microphone.

"I know you think I probably came here from America to impress you with how great I am," I started, waiting for my interpreter to repeat each phrase in Spanish, "but instead, I want to tell you about some things I'm not so good at. First of all, I'm not a very good cook. Actually my husband says it's not that I'm a bad cook but that I just have a very small repertoire." David shrugged his shoulders behind me as they giggled.

"And I can't make anything grow," I told them. "My friends tell me if I would water my plants, the plants would live, but once they're in my house they're kind of on their own and eventually they turn brown."

"And I'm really bad at the laundry," I continued. "I buy my husband a new sweater, and when I wash it, it shrinks. I accidentally wash the white load with something red, and it all comes out pink. Our clothes have spots and stains I just can't seem to get out." You would have thought I was a comedian on Comedy Central; they thought I was so funny.

But then I said, "Just like there are stains that we can't seem to wash out of our clothes, things we just can't seem to get clean, we also have stains in our lives that we can't seem to get clean. We feel dirty on the inside and hopeless that we could ever become clean and new and good again." There was no laughter this time; just heads nodding.

After speaking that day to some of the lowest members of Bogotá's society, the next day I spoke to some of the most respected. The heads of all the military branches, governmental leaders, business leaders, and even Miss Colombia were at Bogotá's most exclusive club for a breakfast. And as I prepared to speak, I realized that many of the people there had the opposite problem from the prostitutes. They had little sense of their need for forgiveness and cleansing because they saw themselves as clean and good already. Whereas the prostitutes saw themselves as too dirty to be accepted by God, these people saw themselves as too clean to have any need for the cleansing that God provides.

And as far apart as the two groups were economically and socially, I realized they had the exact same need that you and I have. We need to see ourselves as God sees us, as sinners in need of forgiveness and reconciliation. And we need to see God as he is, which is full of mercy and compassion for any and all sinners who will cry out to him for forgiveness.

The Bible tells us about someone who was at the very top of his society and so "in" with God that he was called "the man after God's own heart." But because the Bible is not afraid to draw its heroes in the colors of reality, we know that King David also understood what it is to be at the bottom, feeling dirtied by sin and far away from God.

King David was walking on the roof of his house when he saw a beautiful naked woman bathing. And he had to have her. He sent messengers to get her and slept with her and then sent her away. But a short time later she sent David a message, saying, "I'm pregnant" (2 Sam. 11:5).

Have you ever been caught doing something you couldn't cover up or saying something you couldn't take back? Do you remember how it made your heart pound and gave you a sick feeling in your stomach even as you began to try to think of some way to get out of the mess you'd gotten yourself into? (Or am I the only one?) That's what David felt. He went into high gear on his cover-up operation, sending for Bathsheba's husband to come home from the warfront and then sending him home to Bathsheba. David assumed that a man who had been off to war for many months would take advantage of a night at home with his beautiful wife and would then think that her pregnancy resulted from that night he spent at home. But Uriah considered himself still on duty with the rest of his men and slept at the door of the king's house rather than going home to his wife. So David moved on to plan B, getting Uriah drunk in hopes that he'd head home and do what would certainly come naturally with his defenses down. But once again, Uriah did not go home to Bathsheba.

So David took another step deeper into the gutter and wrote a letter to Joab, the commanding officer, instructing that Uriah be abandoned on the frontlines of battle, effectively arranging for his murder. Then David brought Bathsheba to his house and she became his wife. Perhaps he put on a great charade of acting surprised when Bathsheba gave birth to such a healthy-looking boy much less than nine months after their marriage. Maybe David thought he had gotten away with it. He must have wanted to just put it behind him and forge forward. But God loved David too much to let him bury this sin, and he sent Nathan the prophet to David with a story:

> There were two men in a certain city, the one rich and the other poor. The rich man had very many flocks and herds, but the poor man had nothing but one little ewe lamb, which he had bought. And he brought it up, and it grew up with him and with his children. It used to eat of his morsel and drink from his cup and lie in his arms, and it was like a daughter to him. Now there came a traveler to the rich man, and he was unwilling to take one of his own flock or herd to prepare for the guest who had come to him, but he took the poor man's lamb and prepared it for the man who had come to him." Then David's anger was greatly kindled against the

man, and he said to Nathan, "As the LORD lives, the man who has done this deserves to die, and he shall restore the lamb fourfold, because he did this thing, and because he had no pity." Nathan said to David, "You are the man!" (2 Sam.12:1–7)

This was the most devastating and targeted sermon application of all time. Seeing what he had done from another angle enabled David to see the truth about himself. And rather than refuse to hear it or rant against it, David received this devastating indictment, saying to Nathan, "I have sinned against the LORD" (2 Sam. 12:13).

David realized that he had kicked dirt in the face of the one who had chosen him and protected him and empowered him and placed him on the throne. How would he face God after having fallen so far from what God intended for him to do and be? How would he continue as king, having lost his credibility? How would he even continue to look at himself in the mirror everyday?

When we come to Psalm 51, we find out how. The notation indicates it is "a psalm of David, when Nathan the prophet went to him, after he had gone in to Bathsheba." Psalm 51 draws back the curtain so that we are able to look into the interior of David's repentance. In this prayer of repentance, David shows us how a man or woman after God's own heart pursues God and finds the way home when he or she has royally messed things up.

Have Mercy on Me

David began his prayer not by obsessing about his own lack of character but by depending on God's strength of character:

> Have mercy on me, O God,
>> according to your steadfast love;
> according to your abundant mercy
>> blot out my transgressions.
> Wash me thoroughly from my iniquity,
>> and cleanse me from my sin! (Ps. 51:1–2)

You may remember the answer to the question in the Westminster Shorter Catechism for Young Children: "What is prayer?" The answer is,

"Prayer is asking God for things which he has promised to give." That is what David is doing in this prayer. David has not pulled this request for mercy out of thin air. God had revealed long before that he is "a God merciful and gracious, slow to anger, and abounding in steadfast love and faithfulness, keeping steadfast love for thousands, forgiving iniquity and transgression and sin, but who will by no means clear the guilty" (Ex. 34:6–7). From this declaration of God, recorded by Moses, "David knew that there were guilty [people] who would not be forgiven, and there were guilty [people] who, by some mysterious work of redemption, would not be counted as guilty but would be forgiven."[1] In Psalm 51 David is crying out to lay hold of that mysterious mercy through which he could be forgiven rather than condemned.

Likewise he is appealing to God on the terms God has set for dealing with his people—covenant terms. The word translated "steadfast love" is God's "I will love you forever" commitment. While David is well aware of the offense of his sin, he is equally confident in God's unflinching commitment to those who have embraced his covenant from the heart.

Forgive Me

> For I know my transgressions,
>   and my sin is ever before me. (Ps. 51:3)

God brought conviction upon David so that he could no longer ignore his sin. To come under conviction of sin is a gift of God, a confirmation that we are truly his child. It is God's gracious conviction of sin, his making us aware of our guilt, that drives us back into the arms of his grace. Without it, we would linger away from him, our hearts becoming harder, until we no longer feel the pointed sting of conviction.

David has felt that sting. David's sin is "ever before" him. Have you ever gotten a bad haircut and been reminded of it every morning when you look in the mirror, almost startling yourself with the fresh sight of it every day? This is what David is dealing with on a far grander scale. The ugliness of his sin is the first thing he thinks about when he wakes up in the morning. He sees evidence of it and consequences for it everywhere he looks throughout the day and as he drifts off to sleep at night.

He is unable to find a place deep enough to bury it, and at this point he doesn't want to. He realizes that while he violated Bathsheba by using her for his own pleasure, and while he betrayed Uriah by engineering his death, his sin is ultimately against God. Sin, by definition, is against God, since it is only by God's law that sin is defined as sin.

> Against you, you only, have I sinned
> and done what is evil in your sight,
> so that you may be justified in your words
> and blameless in your judgment. (Ps. 51:4)

David is no longer burying his conscience or justifying his actions. Instead, he's saying that God would be justified to damn him forever.

> Behold, I was brought forth in iniquity,
> and in sin did my mother conceive me. (Ps. 51:5)

David is not saying he is a good person who slipped up and did a bad thing but that his sinful acts are the natural outgrowth of his thoroughly sinful nature. He's not saying that his parents were sinning when he was conceived but that his parents were sinners when he was conceived, and that he is a sinner because he is a part of a whole human race of sinners. Sin is the fabric of our humanity, not merely a matter of our life's experience. David knows that he has sinned because he is a sinner. It is what sinners do. But he doesn't want to do it anymore. He wants something else to define him from the inside out.

> Behold, you delight in truth in the inward being,
> and you teach me wisdom in the secret heart. (Ps. 51:6)

David knows that God sees into the core of his being and that what he sees is someone who has experienced the grace of God and yet sinned against that grace. Sin flourishes when lies are cherished in the inward being and when foolishness is entertained in the secret heart. David wants truth from God to replace the lies he's listened to and wisdom from God to replace the foolishness he has tolerated.

Think about the sins that have derailed your life along the way or the sin that continues to nip at your heels, always threatening to take you down again. What lie has taken root in your inward being that propels you to keep saying yes to that sin?

∼ Is it the lie that a little gossip is just having fun?
∼ Is it the lie that a quick look won't hurt anybody?
∼ Have you entertained the foolishness in the secret place of your heart that you'll get serious about reading your Bible when the kids are gone?
∼ Have you let the foolish notion that your constant criticism of your spouse has no effect on your children settle in your secret heart?

Sometimes people do terrible things and then wonder out loud, "How could this happen? I don't know why I did it. It's not like me." What has happened is that the inward reality of a person's life becomes an outward action. Who they really are, what they really believe, and what they really value is exposed by what they do. This is why God desires and delights in inward purity as well as upright conduct.

Our greatest flaws, the sins that are constantly hurting people around us and infecting every area of our lives with poison, are the sins we don't easily see. That's why they have so much power. So how are we going to be made aware of these hidden sins? How are the sins we've swept under the rug of our conscious thoughts ever going to come to light?

You and I need a Nathan. David needed to see himself from a fresh angle to be able to see his sin for what it was. He needed someone who had the courage to talk to him straight, both about the heinousness of his sin and the wideness of God's mercy.

"Do you have any Nathans in your life?"[2] Do you have any friends who love you and want the best for you to whom you give permission on a regular basis to shoot straight with you about the bad attitudes taking shape in your life or the good things that may be becoming idols in your life? Do you welcome the difficult and sometimes awkward truth of a friend, or do you become too easily offended, too angry, or too devastated so that you subtly intimidate anyone who might consider telling you the hard truth? When someone dares to share with you the sin you've been blind to, do you immediately look around for someone who will reassure you that you're really not in the wrong, or do you take a long look in the mirror and carefully and humbly weigh that person's words?

Cleanse Me

When David weighed carefully what Nathan had told him, a sense developed within him that he was unclean and unable to cleanse himself.

> Purge me with hyssop, and I shall be clean;
> > wash me, and I shall be whiter than snow.
> Let me hear joy and gladness;
> > let the bones that you have broken rejoice.
> Hide your face from my sins,
> > and blot out all my iniquities. (Ps. 51:7–9)

Notice the words David used: *purge*, *wash*, *blot out*. To purge is to get rid of something. He wants to have all the files pertaining to his sin erased from the hard drive of his heart. Sin has permeated the deepest part of him, and he knows that only God can deal with this ingrained filth. He wants to be washed vigorously so that he is scrubbed clean. He's saying, *God, scrub me until the dirt is gone for good.* He wants God to "blot out" all of his iniquities. Remember Wite-Out, that bottled magic we so desperately needed for typing a letter or a paper before the invention of personal computers? David wants the mistake he has made to be covered over. He's asking God to cover over the mess that he has made so that a new chapter can be written in his life.

Make Me New

David wants more than to simply be forgiven. He wants to be made new. He wants God to do a transforming work in his life so that he will no longer be that lustful man trolling for elicit sex on the rooftop or that corrupt king who could justify the assassination of one of his most loyal military leaders. He knows he is certain to keep on sinning in this way unless God does what only God can do.

> Create in me a clean heart, O God,
>   and renew a right spirit within me. (Ps. 51:10)

David uses the same word here that Moses used in Genesis for describing God's work of creating something out of nothing. He's asking God for nothing less than a miracle of creation. He wants God to create in him a clean heart that will love what God loves, a heart that will beat with a passion for trusting and pleasing God. And it is here we become convinced that David's repentance is real. He's not just sorry he got caught. He's not content merely with forgiveness. His sin and its effects are so terrible to him that he never wants to fall into such flagrant sin again.

Some of us want to be forgiven but we don't really want to change. We want to get off the hook, but we don't want to set up any barriers against doing again whatever it was. We want to keep our options open. And some of us just don't really believe that we really *can* change. But true repentance brings lasting change. The sign of a truly repentant person is that she wants to be changed by God and empowered by God to forsake the sin that has hurt others and offended God so deeply.

> *The good news of the gospel is that God forgives people who don't deserve it but ask him for it anyway.*

David wants to have a "right spirit" within—to be firmly fixed on pleasing God rather than himself. What he doesn't want is to be cut off from God and from the power that God's Spirit provides to him.

> Cast me not away from your presence,
>   and take not your Holy Spirit from me. (Ps. 51:11)

Perhaps David is thinking about what happened to his predecessor, Saul, remembering that "the Spirit of the LORD departed from Saul" (1 Sam. 16:14). David does not want to lose the power of the Holy Spirit that will enable him to overcome temptation. After what he has done, he knows the weakness of his own nature like never before and therefore his great need for divine help. But the very fact that David is praying this prayer is evidence that God has not taken away the Holy Spirit from David. It is the Spirit of God at work in our lives that gives us any desire at all to be in his presence.

Did you notice that David did not pray about his out-of-control sexual behavior that seemingly got him in this mess? Why isn't he begging God to dampen his sexual desire or increase his sexual restraint? Because David knows that his "sexual sin is a symptom, not the disease."[3] And he knows what he needs most is not restraint but restoration. He needs to be restored to that place of deep enjoyment of all it means to belong to God and have him as savior, king, shepherd, and Father. He needs, as Thomas Chalmers put it, "the expulsive power of a new affection."

> Restore to me the joy of your salvation,
>   and uphold me with a willing spirit. (Ps. 51:12)

David wants to leave behind the misery of his sin and have joy again. And certainly the happiest people on earth are those who have been the most forgiven. What could bring more joy than to know you are guilty and yet hear God say, "Yes, your sins have been blotted out. I will never throw them back in your face. I'm giving you a fresh start and fresh power for saying no the next time." The good news of the gospel is that God forgives people who don't deserve it but ask him for it anyway. And he gives it freely.

But wait a minute. How can God do this? We know God is a just God. In fact we're counting on his being a just God. We want evil in this world to be punished. So on what basis can God show mercy? How can he follow through on his promise to rightly judge sin and yet show mercy to sinners? Let's remember what has happened in David's situation. Bathsheba has been raped.[4] Uriah has been murdered. And the baby will die. This is a heinous series of crimes and consequences. Yet once David has confessed his sin,

> Nathan said to David, "The LORD also has put away your sin; you shall not die." (2 Sam. 12:13)

How can David's sin simply be "put away"? David had committed two sins for which the Mosaic law provided no forgiveness. There was no sacrifice prescribed in the law that would cover adultery or pre-meditated murder. In fact, the law called for the person guilty of these offenses to be put to death. Yet Nathan the prophet, who speaks for God, said that David's sin has been "put away." How can God simply put away David's sin and not make him pay dearly? How can God, as a righteous judge, simply look past rape and murder and rejection of his righteous standard? Is God simply sweeping David's sin under the rug of the universe?

> *David's sin is "put away" only in the sense that it is "put upon" Christ.*

No, he isn't. Not at all. Because David has embraced God's covenant from the heart and has therefore come before him in confession and repentance, God sees David's sin in light of the Promised One who will come and take David's sin upon himself. David's sin is "put away" only in the sense that it is "put upon" Christ. Paul, in his letter to the Romans, spells out exactly how God could be just in "putting away" or "passing over" David's sin:

> For all have sinned and fall short of the glory of God, and are justified by his grace as a gift, through the redemption that is in Christ Jesus, whom God put forward as a propitiation by his blood, to be received by faith. This was to show God's righteousness, because in his divine forbearance he had *passed over* former sins. It was to show his righteousness at the present time, so that he might be just and the justifier of the one who has faith in Jesus. (Rom. 3:23–26)

David put his faith in the Promised One, who would be the innocent and all-sufficient sacrifice, pure enough to cover his guilt. And while David, like the other prophets of the Old Testament, "searched and inquired carefully, inquiring what person or time the Spirit of Christ in them was indicating when he predicted the sufferings of Christ," (1 Pet. 1:10–11), his prayer reveals at least a shadowy understanding of how God can be perfectly just and yet show mercy.

Hyssop was a small plant frequently found growing in the crevices of stone walls. Because of its shape and structure, dried hyssop was used as a small brush. When David prayed, "Purge me with hyssop," he was clearly thinking back to the night in Egypt when the Israelites were told to slay a lamb so that its blood could be spread over the doorpost with hyssop. Later, in the ceremonies of the temple, hyssop was used to sprinkle the blood of sacrificial animals on those who had been healed of infectious skin diseases or been defiled by touching a dead body (Num. 19:18).[5]

So when David cried out to God to purge him with hyssop, he was saying, "God, cleanse me and cover me with the blood of an innocent sacrifice! Accept the death of this innocent sacrifice on my behalf and grant me life. I don't know of any sacrifice that can deal with my blood guilt, but you do, God. So I ask you to take that hyssop and dip it in the blood you know of, and apply that blood to me."[6]

The source of that all-sufficient sacrifice is made clear in Hebrews 9 where we read:

> If the blood of goats and bulls, and the sprinkling of defiled persons with the ashes of a heifer, sanctify for the purification of the flesh, how much more will the blood of Christ, who through the eternal Spirit offered himself without blemish to God, purify our conscience from dead works to serve the living God. (Heb. 9:13–14)

In the blood of this Lamb of God there is deep cleansing that reaches into our inner parts where the blood of all of the other sacrifices could never reach. It reaches to the place where our consciences accuse us and tell us that God would never allow someone so dirty into his holy presence.

When we trace the Old Testament story, we see that God gave his people a system of sacrifices to be offered, and if you are like me for most of my life, you have thought that that was the Old Testament way of atoning for sin. But it becomes clear in several places in the Old Testament that the people of that day knew that the blood of bulls and goats and birds did not have the value to make up for the offense or make them clean before God. Obviously David knew this:

> For you will not delight in sacrifice, or I would give it;
>> you will not be pleased with a burnt offering.
> The sacrifices of God are a broken spirit;
>> a broken and contrite heart, O God, you will not despise. (Ps. 51:16–17)

David was not rejecting the sacrificial system but was rejecting making it a substitute for repentance. The Old Testament sacrificial system was never intended as the ultimate mechanism to deal with the problem of sin but was instituted to give the people a sense of the gravity of sin and the need for accountability for sin and to point to the once-for-all sacrifice to come, the Lamb of God whose sacrifice would be sufficient to put an end to animal sacrifice.

Have you put your faith in this Lamb and asked God to cleanse you with his blood? If not, what is keeping you from crying out to God for forgiveness and cleansing and a fresh start? Do you think yourself too dirty? Is there some stubborn stain on your record that you cannot entrust to the blood of Christ to cleanse? Do you think you need that spot as a reminder to continue punishing yourself, that it would be disingenuous to enjoy the freedom of a new start with a purged record? Do you think so much of your sin and so little of the blood of Christ that you don't believe it can wash away your spot?

> Would you be whiter, much whiter, than snow?
> There's power in the blood, power in the blood.
> Sin stains are lost in its life-giving flow.
> There's wonderful power in the blood.[7]

Or is it your presumed goodness and your prideful pretending that keep you from crying out to God for forgiveness? Have you intentionally shut your eyes to the darkness within your own heart so that you will not have to face the painful truth about your mixed motives, your prideful sense of entitlement, or your cold apathy toward God, so that you will not have to experience the discomfort or humiliation of a broken and contrite heart? Repentance is a redemptive anguish that will wash away all of your contaminating self-righteousness.

Would you be free from your passion and pride?
There's power in the blood, power in the blood.
Come for a cleansing to Calvary's tide.
There's wonderful power in the blood.

Perhaps you have not cried out to God in repentance, asking for a new start, because you love your sin and you don't want to let it go. Or perhaps you are ashamed to try one more time to let it go when you have done that so many times before and come back to it again. The grace of God at work in your life provides not only pardon for sin but power over sin.

Would you be free from the burden of sin?
There's power in the blood, power in the blood.
Would you o'er evil a victory win?
There's wonderful power in the blood.

David knew that. He experienced it. Have you?

Looking Forward:
Nothing Unclean Will Ever Enter It

We live in a world of landfills, slums, environmental disasters, and unsafe drinking water. We dust today and have to dust again tomorrow because the filth of this world is constantly settling onto everything everywhere. But the impurity of the world around us is not the greatest threat to our existence. It is the impurity that has worked its way into our very being that has the power to damn us forever.

When we read John's vision in Revelation of the end of the world as we know it, we see that there are two different groups of people—those who are washed and wearing white robes and have nothing to fear, and those who refused to be washed and have everything to fear. There are those who have hidden themselves *in* the Lamb and those who try to hide *from* the Lamb.

Then the kings of the earth and the great ones and the generals and the rich and the powerful, and everyone, slave and free, hid themselves in the caves and among the rocks of the mountains, calling to the mountains and rocks, "Fall on us and hide us from the face of him who is seated on the throne, and from the wrath of the Lamb, for the great day of their wrath has come, and who can stand?" (Rev. 6:15–17)

Those who persisted in their sin, who saw no need for confession or cleansing, will have no ability to stand before the throne of God and will fall down in terror, hoping the rocks and mountains will fall on top of them. But those who fell on their faces before the Lamb and submitted to his cleansing work will fall down not in terror, hiding from the Lamb, but in adoration, praising the Lamb.

They have washed their robes and made them white in the blood of the Lamb.

"Therefore they are before the throne of God,
    and serve him day and night in his temple;
    and he who sits on the throne will shelter them with his
        presence.
They shall hunger no more, neither thirst anymore;
    the sun shall not strike them,
    nor any scorching heat.
For the Lamb in the midst of the throne will be their shepherd,
    and he will guide them to springs of living water,
and God will wipe away every tear from their eyes."
(Rev. 7:14–17)

Those who have been cleansed have no need for protection *from* the Lamb but will be protected forever *by* the Lamb. The cleansing that began when they first believed will be complete. The blood of Christ that not only covers but also conquers sin will have completed its sanctifying work, and they will live forever in a purified environment as purified people.

The new heaven and new earth will be populated by flagrant but forgiven sinners who have been washed with the only cleansing agent that has the power to eradicate sin and enable us to stand before our holy God: the blood of Christ.

Repentance in the Psalms

Getting the Discussion Going

1. Do you think most people in the world today see themselves as evil people who occasionally do bad things or as good people who occasionally do evil things?

Getting to the Heart of It

2. Throughout the Psalms, "the psalmists speak out of the context of covenant. They speak to God and about God on the basis of being in a covenant relationship with him."[8] This is clear in the first verse of Psalm 51, when David asks for mercy from God "according to your steadfast love." What difference does God's covenant commitment make when we sin?

3. David uses three words to describe his sin: *transgression, iniquity,* and *sin*. What did you learn about those three words in your Personal Bible Study?

4. Can you think of ways we label specific sins that make them seem less like sin?

5. David asks God to "restore to me the joy of your salvation." What is he really asking for, and why do you think he asks for it?

6. When David says to God, "For you will not delight in sacrifice, or I would give it; you will not be pleased with a burnt offering" (Ps. 51:16), he is not saying that God rejects the sacrificial system he established but rather that going through the motions of offering sacrifices is no substitute for genuine faith and repentance. How would you describe true repentance? Is it a feeling, an action, or a decision? Is it an event or a lifestyle? How do we know repentance is real?

7. We tend to think of things that are broken as useless. But David says that God desires a broken spirit and a broken and contrite heart. What kind of brokenness do you think God desires and why does he desire it?

Getting Personal

8. In the Personal Bible Study you were asked what specific sins you have confessed to God in the last week, or month, or year. Sometimes, if we're honest, we have a hard time coming up with sins to confess and a hard time working up any genuine sorrow over them. Has that ever been your experience? And if so, why do you think that is?

Getting How It Fits into the Big Picture

9. Throughout this study we are considering how the particular book we are studying fits into the larger story of God's plan of redemption and his written revelation. How is the question of how God will be both just and merciful answered only through Christ?

The Suffering and Glory of Messiah in the Psalms

The Suffering and Glory of Messiah in the Psalms

After Jesus rose from the dead, he appeared to two disciples on the road to Emmaus who were terribly sad because the one they had thought was the Messiah had been crucified, causing them to conclude that he was not the one they had been waiting for. Jesus then said to them: "O foolish ones, and slow of heart to believe all that the prophets have spoken! Was it not necessary that the Christ should suffer these things and enter into his glory?" (Luke 24:25–26). Jesus was saying that if these disciples really understood and believed what they had read in the Old Testament, they would have known that the Messiah would suffer significantly and emerge from that suffering triumphantly.

One of the passages that should have finally made sense to them after the crucifixion and resurrection of Christ was Psalm 22. In this psalm David describes his own experience of suffering and deliverance, but he was also clearly writing as a prophet, inspired by the Holy Spirit, having been given the ability to see into the suffering of one of his descendants, Jesus, whose suffering would far surpass his own.

1. What is the lament or cry of the psalmist in Psalm 22:1–2?

2. After the psalmist expresses his lament, he expresses hope for deliverance. What is the basis of that hope, according to Psalm 22:3–5?

3. Not only does this sufferer feel abandoned by God, but also he feels tormented by his enemies. Explain how he is tormented, according to Psalm 22:6–8.

4. Once again, the psalmist comes back around to hope. What, according to Psalm 22:9–11, is the basis of his hope?

5. In Psalm 22:12–18 the psalmist describes his enemies and his suffering using both figurative as well as literal ways of expressing his experience. What is the nature and activity of his enemies, according to these verses?

6. What six details does the psalmist give in Psalm 22:14–18 about the physical impact of his suffering?

7. According to Psalm 22:19–21, what does the psalmist want and receive?

8. What similarities do you see in the psalmist's experience described in Psalm 22:1–21 to that of Jesus when he was crucified?

9. In the first half of Psalm 22 the psalmist cries out in complaint, but in verses 22–25, he cries out in another way. What is the nature of his cry in these latter verses?

10. Psalm 22:1–21 is a lonely cry of an individual. In Psalm 22:22–31 the psalmist no longer wants to sing alone but invites "the congregation" to sing along with him in praise to God and celebration of his salvation. List several things the psalmist says will happen because God has delivered him from death.

11. Why, according to Psalm 22:28, is the psalmist confident that these things will occur?

12. Jesus told the disciples that "everything written about me in the Law of Moses and the Prophets and the Psalms must be fulfilled" (Luke 24:44), and then he trained them how to read and understand the familiar books of the Old Testament in light of his fulfillment. Later, the Gospel writers were careful to show how Christ did, in fact, fulfill what was written in the Old Testament. Sometimes they offered commentary, pointing out when Jesus said or did something to fulfill what was written in the Old Testament. Other times they were careful to quote Jesus when Jesus himself said that he was a fulfillment of something written in the Old Testament.

Let's look specifically at instances in which Jesus himself quoted or referenced a psalm, saying that it was about him or his experience (remembering that there are numerous additional instances when the New Testament writers connect Jesus to various Psalms). Read the psalm quote in the first column below, and then read the passage in the second column, noting briefly the setting or situation in which Jesus made clear that he is the one his hearers had been singing about all their lives when they sang that psalm.

"Out of the mouth of babies and infants, you have established strength because of your foes." (Ps. 8:2)	Matt. 21:15–16
"The stone that the builders rejected has become the cornerstone." (Ps. 118:22)	Matt. 21:33–42
"The LORD says to my Lord: 'Sit at my right hand, until I make your enemies your footstool.'" (Ps. 110:1)	Matt. 22:41–45
"Blessed is he who comes in the name of the LORD!" (Ps. 118:26)	Matt. 23:39
"Even my close friend in whom I trusted, who ate my bread, has lifted his heel against me." (Ps. 41:9)	John 13:18
"Those who hate me without cause." (Pss. 35:19; 69:4)	John 15:25
"Appoint a wicked man against him. . . . May his days be few; may another take his office." (Ps. 109:6, 8)	John 17:12
"They gave me poison for food, and for my thirst they gave me sour wine to drink." (Ps. 69:21)	John 19:28–29
"Into your hand I commit my spirit; you have redeemed me, O LORD, faithful God." (Ps. 31:5)	Luke 23:46

Teaching Chapter

Who Is This Song About?

A while ago I saw an interview on *60 Minutes* with Chris Martin, the lead singer of the band Coldplay. Steve Kroft was just starting to ask him about their first worldwide hit song, "Yellow," but before he could get the question out, Martin interrupted, asking the question for him, "What's it about?" Martin continued, "I have no idea. I still think about it every day. I love playing it. I love the tune. I love the chords. I love the balloons we use when we perform it live. But I still can't work out what it's about."

I read one account that said that when they were composing the song's lyrics, there was a word missing, and Chris Martin looked around the studio and saw the yellow pages on the counter and stuck the word "yellow" in where the song needed a word. (And we thought it had this deep meaning that we were supposed to mine.)

This is one of those songs about which we wonder, "*What* is this about?" But there are other songs about which we want to know, "*Who* is this about?"

We have sung along with Carly Simon for years, "You're so vain, I bet you think this song is about you." And we have wondered: *Who flew his Learjet to Nova Scotia to see the total eclipse of the sun?* Evidently, after guarding the secret for thirty-eight years, Carly whispered the first name of the man about two and half minutes into a new version of the song, recorded in 2010, that you can detect if you listen to it backwards. (How exactly you are supposed to do that, I'm not sure.)

Evidently she whispers the name "David." Now we just have to nail down who David is.

Certainly the people of King David's day and the people of God who sang the psalms throughout the years to come must have wondered as they sang certain psalms, *Who is this about? What event is this describing?* Because while there are numerous psalms in which David describes his own experiences so that we know he is referring to specific events in his own life, there are other times when the description goes beyond anything David experienced. David seems to be describing someone else. It seems that someone else's name is being whispered in his words.

We need to remember that David and all the other human authors of the Old Testament were not just writing down their own thoughts and ideas when they wrote the books that would become the Bible. Peter wrote, "No prophecy was ever produced by the will of man, but men spoke from God as they were carried along by the Holy Spirit"(2 Pet. 1:21). The divine author worked through the human authors of the Psalms and the rest of the Old Testament so that they were able to write about things to come that they did not always clearly understand themselves, but wanted to. Peter explained:

> Concerning this salvation, the prophets who prophesied about the grace that was to be yours searched and inquired carefully, inquiring what person or time the Spirit of Christ in them was indicating when he predicted the sufferings of Christ and the subsequent glories. (1 Pet. 1:10–11)

The "Spirit of Christ" in David enabled David and other biblical authors to write about the Christ who would come. Notice that Peter specifically says that the Old Testament writers predicted "the sufferings of Christ and the subsequent glories." It is similar to what Jesus said on the road to Emmaus when he scolded the two disciples who had concluded that, because Jesus had been humiliated by crucifixion, he could not have been the Messiah. At that point, they didn't recognize that it was Jesus who was speaking to them. Jesus said:

> O foolish ones, and slow of heart to believe all that the prophets have spoken! Was it not necessary that the Christ should suffer these things and enter into his glory? (Luke 24:25–26)

Jesus was saying that if they had really taken in what they had been reading in the Old Testament throughout their lives, they would have understood that the Messiah would suffer and then be glorified.

The suffering and subsequent glories of the Messiah are shown in shadow form in David's description of his own experiences. While David wrote about himself and his own experiences in the Psalms, and while some psalms were written about David, we are learning that they are more profoundly about David's greater son to come. Certainly there were aspects to what was written in the Psalms that couldn't be traced to David or any of the other kings who sat on the throne of Israel. So the people of Israel watched and waited and wondered who the songs were about, even as they sang the songs week after week and year after year.

But there was one Jewish boy who grew up singing the Psalms who knew exactly who the Psalms were about. These were the songs Jesus sang. In the Psalms "he found the shape of his own identity and the goal of his own mission."[1] Numerous times while growing up, he quoted and attributed to himself psalms that had always been understood as being about King David. And after his resurrection he was bold enough to say that the entirety of the Psalms was most profoundly all about him.

So far as we've worked our way through the Psalms, while we have really only skimmed the surface of this amazing book, we've found numerous ways in which the Psalms speak of Christ. Because we have a greater understanding of God in three persons than the Old Testament saints had, we know that when the Psalms speak of or are sung to the "LORD," that designation is to the triune God, who is Father, Son, and Spirit. We've seen that Jesus is the ultimate blessed man who delights in the law of the Lord, and he is the Lord's Anointed who will reign forever on David's throne. We've seen that only the sacrificial work of Jesus addresses the tension as to how God can be both just and merciful. And in this, our fifth week on the Psalms, we are going to look at several psalms to see how Christ clearly fulfills the prophetic descriptions of the suffering and glorification of the Messiah.

Song of Rejection

Jesus grew up singing a song about the rejection he would experience. Psalm 118 describes a festive procession into Jerusalem after some great deliverance, which was perhaps originally composed for some special ceremony and sung at the Feast of Tabernacles as well as at Passover. When God's people arrived at the temple gate, the leader would sing from Psalm 118, "Open to me the gates of righteousness, that I may enter through them and give thanks to the LORD" (v. 19). And the people inside the gates would reply, "This is the gate of the LORD; the righteous shall enter through it" (v. 20). Then together they would sing songs of praise to the Lord God. At the heart of this beautiful Hebrew processional song of worship were the words: "The stone that the builders rejected has become the cornerstone" (v. 22).

As the Israelites sang this song, they thought of Abraham and David, as well as of the people of Israel as a whole, as this "rejected stone." Israel was small and despised, held in contempt by the Gentile nations. But when Jesus sang this song, he understood that what was relatively true of the people of Israel was completely true of him. He was rejected with distain by the Jewish "builders"—the teachers of the law, priests, and Pharisees. While we might think that the people who for centuries had longed for their Messiah to come would welcome him gladly when he came, Jesus just wasn't at all what they had come to expect. Between the time of the prophets and the coming of Jesus, expectations of Messiah became loaded with the hopes of a national, political, and even military Jewish restoration, which became even more acute in the days of servitude to the Roman Empire. When Jesus did not fulfill these hopes, he was soundly rejected.

Jesus recognized this rejection by the religious leaders and confronted it by telling a series of parables that indicted them for their rejection, including the parable of the tenants recorded in Matthew 21. The parable tells of a landowner who planted a vineyard, rented it out to tenant farmers, and went on a journey. When harvest time came, the landowner sent his servants to collect his share of the crop, but the farmers beat one of the servants, killed another, and stoned a third. The owner then sent a larger group of servants to collect for him, but the farmers did the same things again. Then he sent his son, thinking, "They will respect my son" (Matt. 21:37). However, the farmers took the heir and killed him. Jesus concluded his parable with the familiar words from Psalm 118:22: "The stone that the builders rejected has become the cornerstone." With this parable, Jesus exposed the guilt of the religious leaders who had rejected and were plotting to kill God's own Son, making clear that he was the rejected stone they had sung about all their lives .

While the religious leaders rejected Jesus, it was one of those closest to him who turned him over to them. This too, we find in the Psalms.

Song of Betrayal

Jesus grew up also singing a song about the betrayal he would experience by Judas. Throughout the Psalms, David entreated God to give him victory over his enemies. But in Psalm 41 David lamented that even his friends were against him: "Even my close friend in whom I trusted, who ate my bread, has lifted his heel against me" (v. 9). David might have been referring to Absalom, the son who had eaten at his own table but violently turned against him later. Whoever the friend-turned-foe, David saw himself as a righteous sufferer facing opposition from malicious enemies who brought false charges against him.

Jesus, who was conscious of his identity as the son of David, used the words of David from Psalm 41 on the night of the last supper with his disciples, saying that he fulfilled them. John writes that "the devil had already put it into the heart of Judas Iscariot, Simon's son, to betray" Jesus (John 13:2) and that Jesus "knew who was to betray him" (v. 11). Jesus said, "The Scripture will be fulfilled, 'He who ate my bread has lifted his heel against me.' I am telling you this now, before it takes place, that when it does take place you may believe that I am he" (vv. 18–19).

Notice in that last passage that Jesus did not quote the entire verse from Psalm 41. He did not include the first part of verse 9 that says, "Even my best friend, the one I trusted completely," because Jesus had always known that Judas had never truly been a trusted friend, that he had the heart and intentions of a betrayer. Jesus used the words of the psalmist to make clear ahead of time that Judas's betrayal did not catch him by surprise.

So when Jesus sang the Psalms, he sang of his own experience of being rejected (Psalm 118) and of being betrayed (Psalm 41). But when he sang Psalm 22, it must have filled his fully human heart with dread.

Song of Desolation

As David wrote Psalm 22, undoubtedly he was reflecting on many of his experiences of feeling abandoned by God, of being surrounded by enemies, and of being exposed, and yet also of being preserved and exalted by the powerful hand of God. But he seems to express his experience of suffering in stretched poetic language, going beyond a literal description of his personal experience into hyperbole that finds literal fulfillment in his greater Son.[2]

Under inspiration of the Holy Spirit, David wrote in Psalm 22 of his descendant whose experience would resemble yet also surpass his own suffering.

Under inspiration of the Holy Spirit, David wrote in Psalm 22 of his descendant whose experience would resemble yet also surpass his own suffering.

We know this for several reasons. First, the pattern of David's experience described in Psalm 22 is identical to the pattern of Jesus's experience. Jesus emphasized this pattern to his two followers on the road to Emmaus—suffering before glory, humiliation followed by exaltation. The first half of Psalm 22 is a vivid portrayal of suffering and humiliation, while the second part is a victorious proclamation of glorious exaltation.

While David may have been writing about his own experience, each of the Gospel writers, as well as the writer of Hebrews, indicates that Psalm 22 is most profoundly about Christ. We'll see it as we go back and forth between the experience of David and that of Jesus as we work our way through this psalm.

Abandoned by God

My God, my God, why have you forsaken me?
Why are you so far from saving me, from the words of my groaning?

O my God, I cry by day, but you do not answer,
   and by night, but I find no rest. (Ps. 22:1–2)

All of his life the psalmist had been taught to believe in a loving God who was near to those who call on him. David had known the Lord as his shepherd, his refuge, and his help in time of need. But when he wrote these words, evidently his experience seemed to contradict his belief. Rather than being near, God seemed "so far" from him.

Whatever David's personal experience of suffering, surely the agony he described in Psalm 22 surely transcended his own experience. Jesus must have been meditating on Psalm 22, written a thousand years before he was born, as he hung on the cross. In it he found the words that gave utterance to his own agony of soul. Matthew records:

At about three o'clock, Jesus called out with a loud voice, "Eli, Eli, lema sabachthani?" which means "My God, my God, why have you abandoned me?" (Matt. 27:46 NLT)

Up to this point Jesus had been beaten and whipped, he'd had thorns pressed into his temples and nails pounded into his hands and feet, and he had not said anything. And then suddenly from the cross he cried out with these words of Psalm 22. Something infinitely more painful than the physical agony he was enduring was taking place—it was the spiritual agony of having the familiar presence of God withdrawn.

At the cross Jesus became sin for us. And because God cannot look upon sin, the Father had to turn away. Out of hatred for sin and love for sinners, that precious fellowship with the Father that Jesus had always enjoyed was broken. Yet once the wrath of God had burned itself out in the very heart of Jesus, it was clear that it was not forever broken. Jesus spoke again from the cross, shouting the words of Psalm 31:5, "Father, into your hands I commit my spirit!" (Luke 23:46). The price for sin was paid and the relationship restored.

Though it pains us, and perhaps confuses us, to think of God's turning away from his own Son, we must see that this alienation was purposeful and profitable. Jesus experienced the alienation from God in those hours that you and I deserve to experience forever, so that we will never have to experience it. While we may sometimes *feel* abandoned by God, we have never been and never will be. Because Jesus was alienated from God as our substitute, we can draw near. Because God turned his face away from Jesus, we can be confident that he will never turn away from us.

Despised by Men

The psalmist's trouble is compounded in that added to the absence of God was the all-too-real presence of enemies.

> But I am a worm and not a man,
>   scorned by mankind and despised by the people.
> All who see me mock me;
>   they make mouths at me; they wag their heads;
> "He trusts in the LORD; let him deliver him;
>   let him rescue him, for he delights in him!" (Ps. 22:6–8)

The most precious things the psalmist believed and preached and sang about were being hurled back in his face. It appeared that this one who had said "God is my helper" was not being helped.

Amazingly, the precise words of Psalm 22:8 were hurled at Jesus as he hung on the cross by the leading priests, teachers of religious law, and elders (although they certainly could not have realized they were quoting Scripture). They mocked Jesus, saying, "He saved others; he cannot save himself. He is the King of Israel; let him come down now from the cross, and we will believe in him. He trusts in God; let God deliver him now, if he desires him. For he said, 'I am the Son of God'" (Matt. 27:42–43). But the way Jesus would rescue Israel was to refuse to be rescued himself. Our great deliverer was not delivered. And while his accusers sought to discredit him with their insults, they ended up proving, by using these prophetic words, that Jesus *was* who they said he *was not*.

The psalmist was able to see that the human opposition he faced was actually something far more sinister and supernatural.

> Many bulls encompass me;
>> strong bulls of Bashan surround me;
> they open wide their mouths at me,
>> like a ravening and roaring lion. (Ps. 22:12–13)

David had the sense of being surrounded by those who wanted to bite and ravage him. He realized that the attack he was experiencing from his enemies was as old as Eden, when Satan attacked God's representative in the world—not as a lion but as a snake. Since the garden, the seed of the woman and the seed of the serpent have been in perpetual hostility. David realized that he was facing hostility of demonic proportions that sought to destroy him.

Clearly Jesus understood this as well, which is why he told the Pharisees who plotted to kill him, "You are of your father the devil, and your will is to do your father's desires" (John 8:44).

Racked with Pain

David then described the physical agony and humiliating derision he experienced at the hands of his Satan-inspired enemies:

> I am poured out like water,
>> and all my bones are out of joint;
> my heart is like wax;
>> it is melted within my breast;
> my strength is dried up like a potsherd,
>> and my tongue sticks to my jaws;
>> you lay me in the dust of death.
>
> For dogs encompass me;
>> a company of evildoers encircles me;
> they have pierced my hands and feet—
> I can count all my bones—
> they stare and gloat over me;
> they divide my garments among them,
>> and for my clothing they cast lots. (Ps. 22:14–18)

Some scholars have suggested that what David is describing here is a sickness. However, it is clearly more descriptive of an execution.[3]

We know more about David's life than perhaps any other person in the Bible, and there is nothing in his life that would warrant this description. David did not undergo execution. And interestingly, Psalm 22 is a detailed description of a form of execution—crucifixion—written a thousand years before it was invented by the Persians and put into widespread use by the Romans. How did David describe in such vivid detail what would not be invented for another one thousand years? The only possible explanation is that offered by Peter in Acts 2: that David, as a prophet, "foresaw and spoke about" the experience of Christ (v. 31). As David suffered, the Holy Spirit gave him insight into the greater suffering and humiliation of his greater son. And as we read it, remembering that the Spirit inspired it and Jesus read it, we are reminded that God knew exactly what would happen on that excruciating day to come.

Psalm 22 fits the experience of Jesus on the cross like a well-fitting glove—his bones jerked out of joint as the cross was dropped into the ground, the dehydration from being exposed in the hot sun, his hands and feet pieced by nails, the staring and gloating of onlookers as he hung unclothed at eye level, and even the dividing of his garments by the soldiers who gambled for them. But even as Jesus experienced this agonizing pain and alienation, he remained confident that it would not last forever, but would give way to victory. How did he know? He knew the whole story of Psalm 22, a story of suffering but also deliverance from the suffering.

Song of Deliverance

The suffering depicted in the first half of Psalm 22 goes far beyond that experienced by any Old Testament figure and becomes understandable in the light of the crucifixion of Christ. And the glory in the second half of Psalm 22 goes far beyond the glorious victory enjoyed by any Old Testament figure and becomes clear in light of the resurrection and reign of Christ.

The psalmist laments his sense of abandonment and call out for help, and then suddenly and without explanation he says, in verse 21,"You have rescued me," or literally, "You have heard me."[4] David has cried out to be delivered, and his cry has been heard and responded to. He has been rescued from his enemies, from the grip of death.

The writer of Hebrews seems to have this part of Psalm 22 in mind when he writes that "Jesus offered up prayers and supplications, with loud cries and tears, to him who was able to save him from death, *and he was heard*" (Heb. 5:7).

Once the psalmist has been rescued, the whole tone of the psalm goes immediately from lonely agony to a huge celebration party. It was an Old Testament custom that when you had called upon God to act and God had answered your prayer, you were not to keep this joy to yourself but were to call all of your neighbors and have a party at which you would get up and tell what God had done for you.[5] This is the delightful picture of the feast that the psalmist calls for in Psalm 22.

> I will tell of your name to my brothers;
>> in the midst of the congregation I will praise you. (Ps. 22:22)

> From you comes my praise in the great congregation;
>> my vows I will perform before those who fear him.
> The afflicted shall eat and be satisfied. (Ps. 22:25–26)

Hebrews helps us to understand the celebration of the "great congregation," making it clear that David went beyond his own experience in writing about this great feast. The writer of Hebrews tells the first-century Christians to whom he was writing that Jesus is not ashamed to call them brothers, and that Christ himself was speaking through David when David wrote, "I will tell of your name to my brothers; in the midst of the congregation I will sing your praise" (Heb. 2:12). Amazingly Hebrews helps us to read Psalm 22 in the light of Christ so that we can hear Jesus himself inviting us to praise.

When we come to the very end of the psalm, we see that the psalmist—and in a far greater way, Jesus—has been delivered from his enemies and from death itself. Desertion and suffering have given way to praise and confidence, and the ultimate reason is found in the last statement of Psalm 22:

> He has done it. (Ps. 22:31)

In Hebrew there is no object for the verb used in that clause of verse

31, so it could be translated simply "It is done" or "It is finished." We know that Jesus, while on the cross, was meditating on Psalm 22 and that all he experienced there was reflected in what David wrote in Psalm 22. After three hours of darkness Jesus cried out the final words of Psalm 22: "It is finished." What was finished? Everything that was needed to accomplish the salvation of sinners and the redemption of a sin-rav- aged creation was accomplished. What David anticipated, Christ fulfilled.

So let's come back to our original question. Who is this song about? Certainly this song is about David and his experience of feeling aban- doned by God even as his enemies encircled him and attacked him. It is about his deliverance from that dark place through which he called his people to praise. But we also realize this song is most profoundly about Christ—about his passion and pain as well as his resurrection and exalta- tion. Sinclair Ferguson says, "The sea of forsakenness into which David was enabled to dip his feet, our Lord Jesus Christ experienced in the full."[6]

And as we think this through, we realize that we need to reconsider how we've read the Psalms for most of our lives. We've made the mis- take of thinking that whoever we are and whatever we're going through, we can find a psalm to fit our need of the moment and easily adapt it to fit our situation, ignoring whatever doesn't seem to fit our intended purposes. Usually when we read "I" in the psalms, we have ourselves in mind. Carly Simon sings, "You're so vain, I bet you think this song is about you." And the awkward truth is that we are so oriented toward making everything about us that we've made ourselves the central char- acter of the Psalms, putting God in a supporting role.

We've read Psalms seeking to make it about our lives and our cir- cumstances, ignoring the fact that we are reading a story that isn't primarily about us, but about someone far more glorious. The Bible unfolds from Genesis to Revelation with a plotline about the person and work of Jesus Christ. And as we grow in our ability to see Jesus at the center of the Psalms, the hope that we find in the Psalms becomes more solid, the promised presence of God becomes more personal, and the help it offers can be more clearly understood.

Do the Psalms speak to us? Absolutely. They give us a voice and vocabulary to cry out to our God in consternation, confession, and celebration. They show us who our king is, remind us of his personal presence with us, and point us toward the day when he will come again in glory. When we begin to read them in light of Christ, they get us thinking about his suffering and not just our own. And when we really see his suffering and the glory that followed, it helps us to trust that one day our suffering will also come to an end and glory will follow.

We do not want to be so vain as to think the greatest songs ever written are all about us. The songs we want to sing in full voice, the songs we want to make sure the whole world hears, the songs we want to sing into eternity are not about our suffering, or our questions, or our experiences. We want to join in the congregation led by our brother Jesus to sing of his suffering and his glorious victory that he intends to share with us. We want to celebrate his sure salvation provided to us and his righteous reign over us. And when we sing his song, we can celebrate that, because God turned away from him, we will never be abandoned. We can sing with confidence that we do not have to keep trying to save ourselves, because "he has done it." It is finished.

Looking Forward: In the Midst of the Congregation

The psalmist calls for a feast in Psalm 22 to celebrate what God has done in delivering him from his enemies when he cried out to him:

I will tell of your name to my brothers;
    in the midst of the congregation I will praise you:
You who fear the LORD, praise him!
    All you offspring of Jacob, glorify him,
    and stand in awe of him, all you offspring of Israel!
For he has not despised or abhorred
    the affliction of the afflicted,
and he has not hidden his face from him,
    but has heard, when he cried to him.
From you comes my praise in the great congregation;

my vows I will perform before those who fear him.
The afflicted shall eat and be satisfied;
    those who seek him shall praise the LORD!
    May your hearts live forever! (Ps. 22:22–26)

He wants to tell everyone gathered about how God delivered him from death. He wants the afflicted to be there so they can enjoy this same salvation and live forever.

The apostle John was given a vision of this great congregation enjoying Psalm 22's lavish feast, which we read about in Revelation:

Then I heard what seemed to be the voice of a great multitude, like the roar of many waters and like the sound of mighty peals of thunder, crying out,

"Hallelujah!
For the Lord our God
    the Almighty reigns." (Rev. 19:6)

Rather than a localized celebration, the table at this feast will cover the entire earth, and all of Christ's brothers—all who have been united to him by faith—will eat and be satisfied. At this grand gathering to come, we will celebrate the universal and eternal conquest of all creation that Christ accomplished as a result of his suffering, which was longed for and prophesied about in Psalm 22:

All the ends of the earth shall remember
    and turn to the LORD,
and all the families of the nations
    shall worship before you. (Ps. 22:27)

The event that brought redemption from the power of death also began the process of the restoration of creation, which will one day be complete, and it will be celebrated with exuberant, worldwide praise. The resurrected King will reign, and his kingdom will extend over all the earth so that all the families of the nations will worship him, and nothing will be left outside of his domain.

This great message of redemption will continue to be proclaimed to future generations until the resurrected King comes again to bring in the full restoration of all things.

Discussion Guide

The Suffering and Glory of Messiah in the Psalms

Getting the Discussion Going

1. Did you happen to notice the note to the choirmaster in the heading of Psalm 22? It says: "According to The Doe of the Dawn." No one really knows for sure what this refers to, though it may be the name of a tune known by the choirmaster. If that is the case, what do you think this tune must have sounded like? Can you think of any song with an appropriate tune for singing these words?

Getting to the Heart of It

2. Psalm 22 opens with the familiar words that we recognize as Christ's cry from the cross, "My God, my God, why have you forsaken me?" We know, of course, that Jesus knew the answer to this question. What would you say is the answer to the question, and since Jesus knew this, why do you think he broke his silence on the cross to utter these words?

3. We know that while God had to turn away when Jesus became sin in our place, he did not abandon Christ completely or permanently. How do we know this?

4. How would you explain to someone how this psalm, written one thousand years before Christ, can be about David's experience but more profoundly about Christ's experience?

5. How do the two parts of this psalm make it an excellent example of what Jesus meant when he told his followers on the road to Emmaus that if they had understood what the prophets had written, they would have known it was necessary for the Christ to suffer and enter into his glory?

6. We know that Jesus was meditating on Psalm 22 on the cross, because he uttered its opening and final words. In antiquity, since there were no chapter numbers, verses, or even titles of books to refer to or quote from in the Psalms, the first line was generally used to refer to the whole poem. So we could think of Jesus hanging on the cross and saying, "Psalm 22 is what is happening here," which would include both the first and the second half of the psalm. Surely Jesus was meditating beyond the suffering of the cross, described in the first half of the psalm, to the glorious and victorious gathering described in the second half. How would this help us to understand "the joy that was set before him" that enabled him to "[endure] the cross, despising the shame" that we read about in Hebrews 12:2?

Getting Personal

7. In the Teaching Chapter we read that although we tend to make ourselves the main character of the Psalms and our experiences and needs the primary plot, Psalms, along with the rest of the Bible, are supremely about God's work of redemption through Jesus Christ. Do you have a favorite psalm that has meant a great deal to you? Would you read some of it for us and tell us what difference it makes to read it while thinking of it as a song Jesus sings with you, as a song you sing to him, or as a song about him?

Getting How It Fits Into the Big Picture

8. Throughout this study we have been considering how what we are studying fits into the larger story of God's plan of redemption and his written revelation. How do Psalm 22 and other psalms that prophesy about the death and resurrection of Christ increase our confidence that God is working out his plan of redemption and can be trusted to bring it to completion in the consummation?

Proverbs

Proverbs

1. What are several purposes for the book of Proverbs that you find in Proverbs 1:2–6 ?

> *To know wisdom, and instruction*
> *To understand the words of insight*
> *To receive instruction in wise dealing*
> *in righteousness, justice, and equity*

Biblical wisdom essentially involves skill in the art of godly living. It applies God's principles to the whole of ordinary life including relationships, the home, work, justice, decisions, attitudes, reactions—everything a person says and even thinks. The wisdom taught in Proverbs is God-centered through and through, teaching shrewd and sound handling of one's affairs in God's world, in submission to God's will.

Throughout the Old Testament we read about the history of God's people. But the book of Proverbs doesn't give us any sense of history except that it is anchored in history. These are "the proverbs of Solomon, son of David, king of Israel" (Prov. 1:1). So obviously we know that while there is certainly wisdom here that will work to some degree for those outside of God's covenant, this is wisdom that is anchored in God and his covenant people. This vital relationship as a foundation for the wisdom in the book of Proverbs is repeated throughout the book.

"The fear of the Lord is the beginning of wisdom and the knowledge of the holy is understanding" prov 9-10

2. Throughout Proverbs is the repeated phrase "the fear of the LORD." What do you think that means?

To acknowledge that God is to be reverenced and that in him is the source of all wisdom, truth, and goodness.

3. How does one grow in the fear of the Lord, according to Proverbs 2:1–8?

By searching for it as hidden treasure (v4)
By seeking for it as silver (v4) By calling on God for insight (3)

4. One of the most pervasive metaphors of the first nine chapters of Proverbs is *derek*, the Hebrew term variously translated as "way," "path," or "road." Skim through Proverbs 2, 3, and 4. How would you summarize the main point the writer of Proverbs reiterates about the "path" or "paths"?

The two paths separate those who walk in the ways of God and those who walk in the ways of man. The path of God is wisdom, but the path of man is foolishness.

5. In addition to this metaphor of two paths, we also find wisdom and folly personified as Madam Folly (2:16–19; 5:1–14; 6:20–35) and Dame Wisdom (1:20–33; 3:13–18; 4:5–9; 8:1–36), or both (7:1–4, 5–27; 9:1–6, 13–18). These chapters are all addressed to a son from a father, and certainly a father wants to teach his son about the kind of woman to pursue and the kind of woman to avoid. According to Proverbs 9, what are these women like and what do they offer?

A wise woman is industrious and teaches other people how to make the most of their time and find knowledge. The woman of folly leads people to ruin and teaches them her own foolish ways.

6. Proverbs speaks of five basic character types: the simple, the fool, the sluggard, the scoffer, and the wise. Note several things you learn about each of these character types from the following verses, looking especially for (1) where this character comes from; (2) the consequences in this way of life; and (3) the way this character can be changed.

The Simple (Naïve)

The simple believes everything,
  but the prudent gives thought to his steps. (Prov. 14:15)

For the simple are killed by their turning away,
  and the complacency of fools destroys them. (Prov. 1:32)

The prudent sees danger and hides himself,
>   but the simple go on and suffer for it. (Prov. 22:3)

"Whoever is simple, let him turn in here!"
>   To him who lacks sense she says,
"Come, eat of my bread
>   and drink of the wine I have mixed.
Leave your simple ways, and live,
>   and walk in the way of insight." (Prov. 9:4–6)

~ Where being simple comes from:

*Being simple comes from rejecting the paths of wisdom.
The simple lack the discernment to know what is wrong and right.*

~ Consequences:

*The simple suffer because they don't recognize danger.
The simple are killed by their turning away from the path*

~ How to change:

*Give thought to your steps and don't believe all.
Protect yoursaf for from the danger of folly.*

The Fool

Folly is bound up in the heart of a child,
>   but the rod of discipline drives it far from him. (Prov. 22:15)

One who is wise is cautious and turns away from evil,
>   but a fool is reckless and careless.
A man of quick temper acts foolishly,
>   and a man of evil devices is hated. (Prov. 14:16–17)

The wise of heart will receive commandments,
>   but a babbling fool will come to ruin. (Prov. 10:8)

~ Where foolishness comes from:

foolish comes from the heart - it is something inborn within us.

~ Consequences:

*The "babbling fool" will suffered and be destroyed.
The evil man will be rejected*

~ How to change:

*Listen to the words of Christ and "receive
Commandments. Turn from paths of wickedness*

The Sluggard

> The sluggard does not plow in the autumn;
>> he will seek at harvest and have nothing. (Prov. 20:4)

> How long will you lie there, O sluggard?
>> When will you arise from your sleep?
> A little sleep, a little slumber,
>> a little folding of the hands to rest,
> and poverty will come upon you like a robber,
>> and want like an armed man. (Prov. 6:9–11)

~ Where laziness comes from:

It comes from a man who puts off what must be done and never actually does anything.

~ Consequences:

He will face poverty / have nothing.

~ How to change:

Be active and do not put off things that must be done.

The Scoffer

> A wise son hears his father's instruction,
>> but a scoffer does not listen to rebuke. (Prov. 13:1)

> Drive out a scoffer, and strife will go out,
>> and quarreling and abuse will cease. (Prov. 22:10)

> Toward the scorners he is scornful,
>> but to the humble he gives favor. (Prov. 3:34)

~ Where scoffing comes from:

A man who cannot bear to bear rebuke of his own folly. He cannot accept correction.

~ Consequences:

He will not receive favor.

~ How to change:

Listen to instruction and be humble.

The Wise

Wisdom from God [handwritten]

> For the LORD gives wisdom; → *wisdom from God* [handwritten]
>> from his mouth come knowledge and understanding;
> he stores up sound wisdom for the upright;
>> he is a shield to those who walk in integrity,
> guarding the paths of justice
>> and watching over the way of his saints. (Prov. 2:6–8)

> The ear that listens to life-giving reproof → *listens to wisdom* [handwritten]
>> will dwell among the wise.
> Whoever ignores instruction despises himself,
>> but he who listens to reproof gains intelligence. → *wise = accepts reproof* [handwritten]
> The fear of the LORD is instruction in wisdom,
>> and humility comes before honor. (Prov. 15:31–33)

> Get wisdom; get insight;
>> do not forget, and do not turn away from the words of my mouth.
> Do not forsake her, and she will keep you;
>> love her, and she will guard you. → *love wisdom* [handwritten]
> The beginning of wisdom is this: Get wisdom, → *search for wisdom* [handwritten]
>> and whatever you get, get insight.
> Prize her highly, and she will exalt you; → *prize wisdom* [handwritten]
>> she will honor you if you embrace her. → *embrace wisdom* [handwritten]
> She will place on your head a graceful garland;
>> she will bestow on you a beautiful crown. (Prov. 4:5–9)

~ Where wisdom comes from:

Wisdom comes from God [handwritten]

~ Consequences:

Being wise, guarded by wisdom, gain intelligence, you will be exalted, you will be given a beautiful crown. [handwritten]

~ How to get more wisdom:

Listen to reproof, seek and embrace wisdom, prize wisdom. [handwritten]

1) [handwritten]

Proverbs itself is basically divided into two parts. The first nine chapters work like a preface that attempts to convince you to read the book by explaining why wisdom is so valuable. *2)* [handwritten] The rest of the book—chapters 10 through 31—are collections of various wise sayings called "proverbs." What is a proverb? A proverb is a short, clear, memorable statement of truth learned through the distillation of extended human experience; for example, "Absence makes the heart grow fonder" or "Honesty is the best policy."

But biblical wisdom steps quite beyond the bounds of practical observations about the world to make clear statements of faith. A biblical proverb is a little model of reality, a short verbal representation of some aspect of our daily lives lived in the fear of the Lord. By picking up a proverb and turning it over and over and looking at it from all angles, we can see something about the reality of how life works in this world.

The short, pithy statements of Proverbs are not always clear to people and are often misunderstood and misused. To rightly understand and apply Proverbs we need to remember several things.

We need to remember that the *proverbs are not promises*. They are generalizations and observations, not automatic rules. They are tendencies, not guarantees. (One proverb that is often assumed to be a promise is Proverbs 22:6.) Proverbs are general statements, not iron-clad certainties, and may not apply in all circumstances. They are not universally or absolutely true. They do, however, offer practical guidance for making wise decisions and living godly lives.

Proverbs often have to do with consequences. Do this, and this will follow. Act wisely and rightly, and you will be rewarded. Act wickedly and foolishly ignore God, and you will face disaster. That is the way God has made the universe. Yet because of the fall, the order of the world has been corrupted. The book of Proverbs sets us up to look for someone to sort out the disorder of the world. We want someone who will put things right and usher in a new order, which is one way Proverbs points us to Christ.

In Proverbs 8 the writer uses a metaphor of a woman named Wisdom to teach about the nature of God's wisdom. And while this Woman Wisdom is not a preincarnate form of the second person of the Trinity, we do know that Jesus is the embodiment of God's wisdom. Because we know that Jesus said that the whole of the Old Testament is about him, we cannot help but see echoes of who he is and what he has done, in the words of Proverbs 8. And when we compare Proverbs 8 with passages about Christ in the New Testament, the connection becomes unavoidable.

7. Compare the wisdom personified in Proverbs 8 with the Word made flesh in the New Testament and write a statement about Jesus in the second column.

"I have counsel and sound wisdom; I have insight; I have strength." (Prov. 8:14)	1 Cor. 1:30 *Christ Jesus became the wisdom of God*
"I love those who love me, and those who seek me diligently find me." (Prov. 8:17)	Matt. 7:7 *Whoever seeks will find all in Christ.*
"The LORD possessed me at the beginning of his work." (Prov. 8:22)	Col. 1:16–17 *Christ is the one who gives me life and is the one to whom I am subject.*
"Ages ago I was set up, at the first, before the beginning of the earth." (Prov. 8:23)	John 1:1 *God was the beginning.*
"When he established the heavens, I was there; when he drew a circle on the face of the deep." (Prov. 8:27)	John 1:1, 3 *Without Christ there is nothing for his in all things. He is the word made flesh. He is the source of all things.*
"I was beside him, like a master workman." (Prov. 8:30)	Heb. 1:2 *God is the creator.*
"I was daily his delight." (Prov. 8:30)	Luke 3:22; 17:24 *Jesus is the Beloved Son He is the Son of God.*
"Blessed are those who keep my ways." (Prov. 8:32)	John 15:10 *You will find love when you abide in Christ who is love*
"Whoever finds me finds life and obtains favor from the LORD, but he who fails to find me injures himself; all who hate me love death." (Prov. 8:35–36)	1 John 5:12 *Our life is Christ and without him we do not have life.*

Teaching Chapter

Wisdom Calling

Is there anything more frustrating than regret over doing or saying something foolish? Do you know what it is like to lie awake at night wishing you had done things differently, gone a different direction, taken a different position? And do you know what it is like to wake up in the morning and feel the sting of remembering something foolish you did or failed to do that you can't seem to undo?

I remember thinking when I was teenager that I had better judgment than most people my age. But I look back at unhealthy relationships I stayed in for too long and unsafe situations I put myself in too many times, and all I can be is grateful for God's providential and protective hand at work in my life.

I can think of times I've kicked myself because of using money foolishly, like when I didn't want to appear cheap or unsophisticated to some salesperson stranger and spent too much on something I really didn't need or was really too expensive.

I can think of too many times when I foolishly opened my mouth and said something, when I should have stayed silent. And the most painful memories of this kind of foolishness come with pictures of the faces of people who were hurt by my injurious words—words that could never, ever be recalled.

I have foolishly put things off and foolishly rushed into things. I have foolishly trusted and been taken advantage of and foolishly failed to trust and missed out. I have foolishly given too much attention to things that were not worthy of the investment and foolishly ignored what was truly deserving of my time and energy.

Most of us, at one time or another, look at ourselves in the mirror and see someone who has been agonizingly foolish. In fact, all of us come by our foolishness quite naturally. This bent toward foolishness goes as far back as our first parents.

While God made humans to be wise and to live our lives on the proper foundation of loving obedience to him, Adam and Eve made the granddaddy of foolish choices. When they chose to disobey God's prohibition, thinking it would make them wise, it actually turned our race into fools. Foolishness became the default setting for every child ever born.

But God is too good to leave us floundering in our foolishness. He comes to us offering wisdom. But it is more active than that:

> Wisdom cries aloud in the street,
>   in the markets she raises her voice. (Prov. 1:20)

God is not just quietly making the offer of wisdom known; he is standing on the back of a flatbed truck waving his hands, trying to get us to stop barreling down the highway of our way of life and choosing our own way of thinking about things, pointing us in another direction. While the road we are on may be wide and smooth with plenty of company and enticements to keep us heading in that direction, he knows what is at the end of that road. He wants to save us from ending up where that road will take us and from having to endure the pain of regret along the way. He wants us to find our way home—to him. He wants us to take the way that leads back to the life Adam and Eve once enjoyed in his garden, living in the abundance of his provision and presence. But there is only one way to get there.

In our world today many people like to think that all roads—especially all religious roads—ultimately end up at the same destination. We hear all the time that if you are spiritual and sincere, then you will end up in the same place as every other spiritually sincere person. Many people are deeply offended when it is suggested that a person who has the pedal to the metal, driving in the opposite direction from the God of the Bible throughout this life, will not find him at his or her destination in the end. Many people want to close their eyes to the consequences of their choices in this life. In fact, they don't want to be forced to choose. They see no need for choosing. They drift through life resenting the suggestion that there are really only two paths in this life—one that leads to death and misery, and one that leads to life and joy. They refuse to believe that reality could be this black-and-white.

Yet here is God, in the pages of the Bible, and especially in the book of Proverbs, calling out from the highest heights, insisting that there is no middle route between right and wrong, no reasonable compromise between wisdom and foolishness. He comes to us offering exactly what we need to navigate life in such a way that we will enjoy his presence along the away and find him fully at our final destination.

You and I would have to be fools not to want to know this God, to reject his wisdom for navigating our uneven emotions, our unhealthy dependencies, our family dynamics, our social situations, our workaday world. You and I have the God who created us and made the world we are living in, crying out to us, *Do you want skill for life? Here it is. I will lead you and guide you to where you want most to go.*

In the book of Proverbs, God offers us wisdom for the most ordinary and the most important aspects of navigating life in his world as one who belongs to him. By listening to him we can avoid both the here-and-now "I've been a fool!" experiences, as well as the ultimate "I've been a fool!" experience—the one from which there is no recovery, no ability to turn back.

Wisdom Comes from God Himself

Proverbs 1 begins by revealing the human source of this collection of wisdom:

> The proverbs of Solomon, son of David, king of Israel. (Prov. 1:1)

Solomon is portrayed in the Bible as one of the wisest men who ever lived. And it appears that his wisdom was not merely a natural gift but was supernaturally bestowed upon him by God. In 1 Kings 3 we read that God told Solomon he could ask for whatever he wanted and that he would give it to him. And Solomon was at least smart enough to ask for wisdom. So when we open the book of Proverbs and read in the first verse that we are about to read "the proverbs of Solomon," we realize that we are going to be reading wisdom that has been given by God himself.

What is this wisdom that comes from God? It is more than mental prowess or moral goodness. To be wise is not the same as to be smart. Wisdom is skill, expertise, competence, and understanding of how life works. In verses 2–6 of the first chapter of Proverbs we discover the purpose or effect of the wisdom of God contained in Solomon's proverbs:

> To know wisdom and instruction,
>   to understand words of insight,
> to receive instruction in wise dealing,
>   in righteousness, justice, and equity;
> to give prudence to the simple,
>   knowledge and discretion to the youth—
> Let the wise hear and increase in learning,
>   and the one who understands obtain guidance,
> to understand a proverb and a saying,
>   the words of the wise and their riddles. (Prov. 1:2–6)

In these five verses the writer of Proverbs is showing us the benefits of wisdom from a number of different angles, using seven key words for wisdom with various shades of meaning.

Instruction. To be wise, we have to be humble enough to admit we don't know everything and allow ourselves to be taught. Perhaps this seems simple, but so much of our deep foolishness works its way out in prideful resistance to being instructed. James, the New Testament writer about wisdom, wrote: "Receive with meekness the implanted word, which is able to save your souls" (James 1:21). Are you humble enough to let the Bible instruct you, contradict you, show you where you're wrong?

Insight. To have insight is to be able to see what the real issue is, to see beneath the surface of things. Have you ever been on a committee or in a group when someone is able to articulate the real issue that everyone else has been talking around and thought, *That's it!* This is a person with insight. This is someone who "gets it."

Wise dealing. This is the person who knows how to negotiate life in a fallen world filled with sinful people, leaving a trail of healthy rather than ruined relationships and building a reputation for integrity along the way. He does what is right and good and fair. He builds up rather than tears down.

Prudence. Later in Proverbs we read, "The prudent sees danger and hides himself, but the simple go on and suffer for it" (Prov. 27:12). So we see that prudence is the ability to look down the road and see the consequences of a particular choice. Have you ever seen someone (or have you ever been someone) who has found himself or herself in a tangled mess of hurt and destruction and says, "I never dreamed it would lead to this"? To be prudent is to know where certain paths lead and to avoid those that lead where you do not want to go. Prudence allows you to see beyond the immediate gratification of the choices before you to their ultimate consequences.

Knowledge. This is more than someone who merely knows the facts; it is someone who has internalized God's ways. Think for a minute about how the Bible speaks of knowledge, as in Adam "knew" his wife and she conceived. Or think of the husband and wife who know instinctively what the other is thinking. This knowledge is a deep knowing that comes from intimacy. The person who has this kind of knowledge has developed an ongoing intimacy with God so that he or she increasingly knows instinctively what God wants.

Discretion. This is the ability to see through what is false and to resist what is wrong, to commit oneself to a course of action that will produce a result that brings glory to God. This is a person who is not easily fooled by flashy pretense or clever arguments or manipulative tactics.

Learning. This is someone who is teachable, who never becomes a know-it-all, who continues to make fresh discoveries in the Scripture that cause her to change her mind and adjust her course. She listens to other people and learns rather than always being the expert in the conversation.

These seven words Proverbs uses to describe wisdom reveal just what God wants to give us—instruction, insight, wise dealing, prudence, knowledge, discretion, learning. Are you interested? Do you have need of such wisdom? Or do you think that you have life figured out on your own? Do you prefer other counselors, other voices, other sources of insight into how life works?

God has launched an advertising campaign for the wisdom he makes available to all. He has put up billboards on the interstate and flashing ads on the Internet and stuffed flyers into the mailbox of your mind so that you will see your need for wisdom and come to him to get it.

Wisdom Begins with Holy Fear

Proverbs 1:7 assumes that you have signed on the dotted line to take God up on his offer and proceeds to tell you where a life of wisdom begins. This is the universal starting point for anyone and everyone who wants to be truly wise. No one finds the path to wisdom without crossing through this threshold.

> The fear of the LORD is the beginning of knowledge;
>> fools despise wisdom and instruction. (Prov. 1:7)

We can do all of the wise things Proverbs teaches regarding saving our money and working hard and being a faithful spouse and a loyal friend, but if we do not begin here, with the fear of the Lord, we cannot expect to find our way on the path of wisdom.

If the fear of the Lord is the starting place, then we must figure out what it means to fear the Lord.

Hebrew poetry is written in parallel lines—an A-line, then a B-line. And the second line helps us understand the first line. So how does the B-line help us understand what it means to fear the Lord? Evidently, while wise people fear the Lord, fools despise wisdom. *Despise* is not an emotionally neutral word. This is the picture of a person who is far beyond a take-it-or-leave-it attitude toward the wisdom only God provides and arrogantly and antagonistically has contempt for it. So to fear the Lord is the opposite extreme of contempt. It is to humbly and openly put oneself under God's authority and to desire his wisdom and instruction with eagerness and intensity. To fear the Lord is to open our lives under the gracious rule of God rather than throw off his reign of authority. It is to take his generous lovingkindness into our hearts rather than throw it back in his face as unneeded and unnecessary.

> *This desire to know God and respond to him rightly is the driving force of the wise person's life, his or her functional center.*

Throughout Proverbs we are taught about family and friendships and money and work and life and death. But this knowledge becomes beneficial to us only if it is built on this foundation of the fear of the Lord. The fear of the Lord is not simply a pursuit we add to our lives along with our interests in sports and the stock market and Sudoku and celebrities. This desire to know God and respond to him rightly is the driving force of the wise person's life, his or her functional center. The fear of the Lord is not simply the beginning of wisdom but, in fact, all wisdom flows from it like a river flows from a spring. This wisdom goes beyond knowing and doing the Word of God to having a sensitive, mature judgment or discernment of how the fear of the Lord should work itself out in all the circumstances that are not specifically dealt with in the Bible.

Wisdom Invites All to Walk in Its Way

While Proverbs is given to us in God's Word so that we might find the wisdom that God offers, the book of Proverbs is not actually addressed to us, the reader. Reading Proverbs, we get to listen in on a father giving advice to his son about how to live life successfully and avoid its pitfalls along the way. Throughout its chapters, the father points out to the son that there are two "ways" or two "paths" open to him and that he will have to choose one or the other.

One path is the way of wisdom, which leads to life in its fullest sense (Prov. 4:11; 9:1). God is with those who walk this path. "He is a shield to those who walk in integrity, guarding the paths of justice and watching over the way of his saints" (Prov. 2:7–8). Those who walk on this path find it straight and secure and leading to a blessed life.

The other path is the way of folly. This path is called "dark" (Prov. 2:13) and "crooked" (Prov. 2:15). Its dangers include evil people who take pleasure in doing wrong, and hidden snares that may appear good but ultimately only bring harm. Most significant, however, is this path's destination—death and destruction. "There is a way that seems right to a man, but its end is the way to death" (Prov. 14:12).

The most important question we must ask ourselves and answer is this: Which path am I on? The question is not, Which path do I want to be on? or, Which path do I know is the right choice? Those are theoretical questions, and we have to examine reality. If you are honest about the choices you are making with what to do with your time and money, with the choices about where you are investing your emotions and affections, which path are you pursuing? Because the path we are actually walking on will determine our destination.

Last semester my son Matt finished up his final exams and then got in his car to drive home to Nashville from Knoxville. Tired from late-night study sessions, he looked up at one point and saw he was a few miles away from Chattanooga. Somewhere between Knoxville and Nashville the interstate splits and takes those in the left lane south to Chattanooga. He learned that you can't drive down the path to Chattanooga and end up in Nashville even if you think you are headed toward Nashville.

Your direction will determine your destination. We can never think we can pursue the path of pornography and end up in a pure relationship. We can't cut corners at every step and become a person of integrity. We can't continue to chase after the next new thing and end up a contented person.

Solomon, in pointing out the choice we must make between two paths, was wise. But the day came when a man stood among the supposed wise men of his day, the scribes and Pharisees, and said, "Something greater than Solomon is here" (Matt. 12:42). Wisdom greater than that of Solomon was in their midst, and he, too, spoke of two paths:

> Enter by the narrow gate. For the gate is wide and the way is easy that leads to destruction, and those who enter by it are many. For the gate is narrow and the way is hard that leads to life, and those who find it are few. (Matt. 7:13–14)

Jesus warned that people cannot serve two masters. He spoke of healthy trees and diseased trees; sheep and goats; and two builders, one who was wise and one who was foolish. And the deciding factor between each of these paths and pairs was not their wise choices in a general sense but their response to him.

Jesus defined that way of wisdom described in Proverbs in personal terms. He said, "I am the way, and the truth, and the life. No one comes to the Father except through me" (John 14:6). The decision that determines our destination, as Jesus makes clear, is not merely a matter of behavior or companions or intentions, but a matter of how we respond to him, whether we will choose him as our path, our life.

Wisdom Enjoys Its Creation

In fact, if we listen closely, we can hear echoes of Jesus speaking in Proverbs, especially in Proverbs 8 in which the writer gives wisdom human characteristics and a voice to speak. The writer begins to talk about wisdom in the same way we might talk about a ship or a country, calling wisdom a "she." It is as if wisdom has pulled out her résumé to commend herself to us so that we will listen to her and accept her guidance, as if she is saying, *Take a look at my credentials and see if you deem me worthy of listening to.*[1] At the top of her résumé is her date of birth:

> The LORD possessed me at the beginning of his work,
>   the first of his acts of old.
> Ages ago I was set up,
>   at the first, before the beginning of the earth.
> When there were no depths I was brought forth,
>   when there were no springs abounding with water.
> Before the mountains had been shaped,
>   before the hills, I was brought forth,
> before he had made the earth with its fields,
>   or the first of the dust of the world. (Prov. 8:22–26)

She was born before the universe was made. We've never seen this on a résumé before. She was there with the Creator before a speck of mat-

ter was made, before the "in the beginning" of Genesis 1. Next she lists
some of her previous experience:

> When he established the heavens, I was there;
>> when he drew a circle on the face of the deep,
> when he made firm the skies above,
>> when he established the fountains of the deep,
> when he assigned to the sea its limit,
>> so that the waters might not transgress his command. (Prov. 8:27–29)

When we want to know about something significant that has happened, we want to hear from an eyewitness, someone who witnessed
events firsthand. And that is Wisdom. Her experience includes watching the Creator draw the line of the horizon across the sky, dig the ocean
depths, and install its fountains of water. *I was there,* she says. *I was there
when there was just emptiness, and I was there when everything that is came
into being. I know how it was all made. I understand the architecture of the
universe. I know the intricacies of human beings. I know what is underneath
everything that can't be seen by the human eye and what is above everything
that can't be seen by the most powerful telescope.* This is impressive.

Next she lists her skills:

> When he marked out the foundations of the earth,
>> then I was beside him, like a master workman. (Prov. 8:29–30)

She is a craftsman at the Creator's right hand, directing the project,
making sure everything falls into place. This wisdom was the agent of
creation who carried out the Creator's plans for his world.

Then she lists her personal likes and interests:

> And I was daily his delight,
>> rejoicing before him always,
> rejoicing in his inhabited world
>> and delighting in the children of man. (Prov. 8:30–31)

Wisdom says, I am never happier than when I am in the presence of
the Creator, enjoying his creation and the ones he created to enjoy his

world. When we raise songs of grateful praise to our Creator for the world he has made, they are but an echo of Wisdom's song.

This applicant for giving us counsel has our attention. The wisdom that created the heavens and the earth is being offered to us for our benefit in navigating the details of life in this world, and we would be fools not to listen. But who is this really about? How can we come to know this wisdom?

We know that in poetry, human attributes are often personified, such as when the psalmist writes that "righteousness and peace kiss each other" (Ps. 85:10). In Proverbs 8, we are reading dramatic poetry in which an attribute of God—wisdom—is being personified.[2] But we also know that the wisdom that made the world did become a person. The one who was the eternal delight of his Father emptied himself into flesh to become the incarnation of God's wisdom.

> *The wisdom that made the world did become a person. The one who was the eternal delight of his Father emptied itself into flesh to become the incarnation of God's wisdom.*

From the earliest accounts of Jesus, when he stayed behind in the synagogue to discuss theology with the teachers of the law, even though he was only twelve years old, "all who heard him were amazed at his understanding and his answers" (Luke 2:47). Jesus "grew in wisdom and in stature and in favor with God and all the people" (Luke 2:52 NLT). Throughout his teaching ministry, one of Jesus's primary teaching methods was the parable. The Greek word translated as "parable" in the New Testament comes from the Hebrew word for "proverb." In the form and content of many of his sayings, Jesus followed in the traditions of Israel's wisdom teachers.

In Matthew 11 Jesus addressed his opponents who thought John the Baptist was too austere and that Jesus enjoyed parties too much. Listen to what he suggested about himself by his reply:

> For John came neither eating nor drinking, and they say, "He has a demon." The Son of Man came eating and drinking, and they say, "Look at him! A glutton and a drunkard, a friend of tax collectors and sinners!" *Yet wisdom is justified by her deeds.* (Matt. 11:18–19)

Jesus also personified wisdom as a female, just like Proverbs 8 does, clearly applying it to himself.

The essence of the wisdom presented in Proverbs became seeable and knowable and touchable when Jesus became flesh. Christ "became to us wisdom from God" (1 Cor. 1:30), and in him "are hidden all the treasures of wisdom and knowledge" (Col. 2:3). And once we have seen the living wisdom of God in the person of Jesus, it sheds a new light on the wisdom being offered to us, the wisdom speaking to us in Proverbs, and we can never read Proverbs the same way again.

> Blessed is the one who listens to me,
>> watching daily at my gates,
>> waiting beside my doors.
> For whoever finds me finds life
>> and obtains favor from the LORD,
> but he who fails to find me injures himself;
>> all who hate me love death. (Prov. 8:34–36)

We cannot help but hear in these words the words of Jesus, the ultimate wisdom teacher, who said:

> Truly, truly, I say to you, whoever hears my word and believes him who sent me has eternal life. He does not come into judgment, but has passed from death to life. (John 5:24)

John later wrote about Jesus:

> Whoever has the Son has life; whoever does not have the Son of God does not have life. (1 John 5:12).

Clearly, to listen to wisdom is to hear the word of Christ. To find wisdom is to believe in Christ. To be wise is to have the mind of Christ. The favor from the Lord that is obtained by those who find wisdom is "the grace of God . . . given you in Christ Jesus" (1 Cor. 1:4). To hear wisdom calling is to hear Jesus standing on the back of that flat-bed truck saying, "Come to me, all who labor and are heavy laden, and I will give you rest" (Matt. 11:28).

I know you likely think of yourself as a smart person, a savvy person. And I'm quite sure you are. But are you a wise person? You are truly wise only if you have embraced the incarnation of God's wisdom, Jesus Christ. But you must know that this is more than just admiring his teaching or following his example. To embrace the wisdom of God in the person of Jesus means coming to his cross, the supreme demonstration of the wisdom of God.

Wisdom Culminates in the Cross of Christ

Paul presents the cross of Christ exactly this way, as the power and wisdom of God:

> For the word of the cross is folly to those who are perishing, but to us who are being saved it is the power of God. . . . We preach Christ crucified . . . the power of God and the wisdom of God. (1 Cor. 1:18, 23–24)

Notice that, similar to what we've been reading in Proverbs and in the teaching of Jesus, Paul divides life and those who live it into two and only two categories—those who are perishing and those who are being saved. In fact, Paul, a very learned man living in the midst of a culture that valued philosophy and rhetoric, recognized that all of the world's knowledge and know-how is useless apart from Christ. He had no desire to be wise on the world's terms. Instead he said:

> For I decided to know nothing among you except Jesus Christ and him crucified. (1 Cor. 2:2)

To have a perfect SAT score, a high IQ, a record completion time on the *New York Times* crossword puzzle, or even an impeccable track record of success in life is not true wisdom. In comparison to knowing Christ, nothing else is much worth knowing. When it comes down to it, there is really one supreme thing we must know to be wise and live, and that is to know Jesus Christ and him crucified.

You don't have to know everything or have everything figured out to be wise. Jesus makes foolish people wise by filling them with himself. Just as Jesus is our righteousness, so is he our wisdom. Just as the Holy Spirit is at work in us, sanctifying us and making us truly and wholly righteous, so is the Spirit of God working in us, illuminating the written Word so that "we have the mind of Christ" (1 Cor. 2:16) and are therefore wise.

There are really only two paths in this life. And they do not end up in the same place. Only one path avoids the agony of waking up in a place you do not want to be, wondering how you could have been such a fool. Jesus is calling you to the path that leads to the life that is found only in him, saying, "Blessed is the one who listens to me. . . . For whoever finds me finds life and obtains favor from the LORD" (Prov. 8:34–35).

Looking Forward: Ready and Waiting

Just as Proverbs repeatedly speaks of two ways—the way of wisdom and the way of folly—and the two destinations these paths lead to, Jesus repeatedly spoke in terms of two choices, two paths, two kinds of people, and two dramatically different ends. And while Proverbs speaks of these two very different ends with words such as "security" or "disaster" (Proverbs 1), "inhabiting the land" or being "cut off from the land" (Proverbs 2), "scorn" or "favor," and "honor" or "disgrace" (Proverbs 3), and "life" or "death" (Proverbs 8), Jesus also used proverbial stories to illustrate the starkly different futures of those who wisely place their hopes in him, and those who foolishly put their hopes in the things of this world.

Specifically, in Matthew 24 and 25, Jesus spoke of the different futures of those who are chosen, alert, faithful, waiting, and watching for his second coming and those who are not. "Two men will be in the field; one will be taken and left. Two women will be grinding at the mill; one will be taken and one left" (Matt. 24:40–41). He spoke of the faithful and wise servant who was placed in charge of all his master's possessions, and contrasted him with the wicked servant who acts foolishly in not expecting his master to return so that he is consigned to "that place" where "there will be weeping and gnashing of teeth" (Matt. 24:45–51).

Jesus continued his theme of the wise watching for his return and the foolish being unprepared by telling a parable:

> Then the kingdom of heaven will be like ten virgins who took their lamps and went to meet the bridegroom. Five of them were foolish, and five were wise. For when the foolish took their lamps, they took no oil with them, but the wise took flasks of oil with their lamps. As the bridegroom was delayed, they all became drowsy and slept. But at midnight there was a cry, "Here is the bridegroom! Come out to meet him." Then all those virgins rose and trimmed their lamps. And the foolish said to the wise, "Give us some of your oil, for our lamps are going out." But the wise answered, saying, "Since there will not be enough for us and for you, go rather to the dealers and buy for yourselves." And while they were going to buy, the bridegroom came, and those who were ready went in with him to the marriage feast, and the door was shut. Afterward the other virgins came also, saying, "Lord, lord, open to us." But he answered, "Truly, I say to you, I do not know you." Watch therefore, for you know neither the day nor the hour. (Matt. 25:1–13)

Evidently all ten virgins had been invited to take part in the wedding celebration, and from all outward appearances they are alike. The only thing that sets them apart from one another is that some had oil for their lamps and some did not. Without trying to allegorize every part of the parable, we recognize that the big picture of the parable is that these foolish virgins were not prepared for the coming of the bridegroom. And their lack of preparedness is tragic. While they are off buying more oil, the feast began, and the door was shut. They had been invited, and they were sure there had to be a place for them. They don't seem to have done anything evil. Yet the door was shut in their faces. They are sure that there must be a way for them to get in, so they plead with the bridegroom.

When Jesus puts the phrase "Truly, I say to you" in this parable, he emphasizes that the words to follow are vitally important. The words that follow—"I don't know you"—are devastating. These foolish virgins had expected to be lifting their lamps high, enjoying the celebration, but their failure to be ready when the time came meant that they were excluded finally and forever.

Jesus was warning that those who foolishly do not prepare for his coming do not know him, and more significantly for their eternal future, he does not know them. The basis for their rejection is not their foolish behavior but their foolish rejection. The issue is relationship to the bridegroom Jesus. They never had a real relationship with him through obedient, living, personal faith. And nonreadiness on that day is without remedy.

There is only one way to be ready, and the wise will heed this warning: the fear of the Lord is the beginning of wisdom. The fear of the Lord produces in us longing for relationship with Christ as we wait in expectation and readiness for his coming.

Discussion Guide

Proverbs

Getting the Discussion Going

1. What makes the proverbs effective is that they are short and easy to remember. Can you recall a proverb from the book of Proverbs or at least the gist of it?

Getting to the Heart of It

2. Think of someone you know whom you think of as a wise person. What is it about that person that causes you to think of him or her as wise?

3. How do you think a person becomes wise or increases in wisdom? Is it something a person can pursue or develop, or is it simply a matter of personality type or disposition?

4. The Old Testament speaks of the fear of the Lord as the beginning of wisdom. How would you put that in New Testament terms? What would you say is the beginning of wisdom now that we know the triune God in a fuller way?

5. Proverbs is full of insight on how to use money, how to deal with people, and how to be successful in this life. Is this insight of benefit to those who do not fear the Lord?

6. After studying Proverbs, how would you respond to someone who insists that all paths lead to God as long as one is sincere?

7. Is it possible to be wise and yet reject Christ?

8. Many people in our world today can make no sense of belief in a god who was publically executed. Certainly the Greeks of Paul's day saw it as utter foolishness. Yet Paul describes the crucifixion of Christ as the power and wisdom of God. What do you think that means?

Getting Personal

9. Throughout Proverbs we've seen that, to be wise, a person needs to receive instruction and learn. So teachability is an important quality of a wise person. Do you think you are a teachable person? Would those closest to you describe you as teachable? Why or why not?

10. Many of us live with lingering regret over foolish things we have done or failed to do, and so we are grateful for the healing, forgiving, restoring grace of Jesus Christ. What difference does it make, or could it make, to truly grasp what it means that Christ has become your wisdom as you are united to him?

Getting How It Fits into the Big Picture

11. In the beginning of the Bible we witness a perfectly ordered universe where actions had predictable consequences. That order was disrupted, yet not completely destroyed when sin entered into the world. And while Christ has accomplished what is necessary for perfect order to be reestablished, all will not be set completely right until Christ returns and the old order passes away for good. Proverbs helps us to see that there is still *some* order in the world we are living in. How does Proverbs also help us as people who are living in this in-between time as we wait for perfect order to be restored?

Week 9

Ecclesiastes

Personal Bible Study

Ecclesiastes

Do you have questions about how life in this world works, quandaries about some of its unfair agonies as well as its unexpected joys? So did the writer of the book of Ecclesiastes, and through this book, he invites us into his questions as well as a few of his conclusions. This book is not easily understood. Nor is it a book from which we can pluck out a verse or two and attempt to hang our whole theology on it. But certainly the key way to approach this book is to seek to understand its purpose and its place within the wisdom books of the Old Testament. To do that, we have to go back to the very beginning of things.

1. When God created everything in the beginning, it was "very good" (Gen. 1:31). But when Adam and Eve fell from the perfect state in which they were created, everything changed. Fulfillment changed to futility. What signs of fulfillment becoming futility do you find in Genesis 3:14–19?

2. In Ecclesiastes 1:2 and, in fact, thirty-eight times throughout the book, the author will describe all of life as "vanity." What does *vanity* mean? (You may want to use a dictionary.)

3. Read the introduction to Ecclesiastes in 1:2–11. Think about the images used and the questions asked. How would you summarize the preacher's assumptions about life?

4. Read Ecclesiastes 1–2 and 3:16–4:16. List five or more things the preacher determines are "vanity."

5. Many interpreters say that the repeated phrase "under the sun" means a life apart from relationship with God. Yet several passages talk about life "under the sun" in relationship with God (Eccles. 5:13–20; 8:14–15; 9:9). What conclusions do you come to about what the writer is referring to when he talks about "under the sun" in Ecclesiastes 1:14–15; 3:16; 6:12; and 9:3–6?

6. The New Testament also speaks to life in this world "under the sun." What is its estimation of it according to these verses?

～ Matthew 6:19–20:

～ 1 Timothy 4:8:

～ 1 Timothy 6:7:

7. In Ecclesiastes 12:9–14 an editor or narrator makes some concluding comments about what "the Preacher" has said throughout the book of Ecclesiastes. Put into your own words what you think he is trying to express to "my son," the one to whom he appears to be speaking in verses 9–12.

8. The narrator's final conclusion is to "fear God and keep his commandments" (Eccles. 12:13). Considering the content and struggle of Ecclesiastes, how is this a necessary resolution and a fitting conclusion?

9. What are the two reasons the narrator gives in Ecclesiastes 12:13–14 for fearing God and keeping his commandments?

10. Is the answer in Ecclesiastes 12:13–14 a satisfying or unsatisfying ending to this book for you? Why?

11. One way we see Christ in the Old Testament is that the Old Testament raises questions that can be answered only in Jesus Christ. And clearly Ecclesiastes raises plenty of questions: Does life in this world have any real meaning? Is there anything worth working toward in this life? Anything worth knowing? Any truth worthy of being believed? Is there anything I can be sure of about life except death?

Of course, we have revelation that the writer of Ecclesiastes did not have—the entire New Testament, which reveals the person and work of Christ. The obvious need of man for whom "everything is futility" (under the sun) is an existence not under the sun. How is this possible and what do we learn about it from these verses in the New Testament?

∼ Romans 5:12, 17

∼ Romans 8:20–23

∼ 1 Corinthians 15:17–19, 58

∼ 2 Corinthians 5:17

∼ Philippians 2:16

∼ Revelation 14:13

Teaching Chapter

What Really Matters

There are lots of things about this life that don't really matter to me. I don't care if the banquet or airline dinner is chicken or beef. I don't care if the deliveryman shows up early or late. I don't care if you call or e-mail. But some things really do matter to me. It matters if the bus driver is drunk or sober. It matters if the lab results are negative or positive. It matters if something costs $1 or $1,000. Certainly some things matter. But what? And why?

We ask ourselves:

> Does it matter if I use Oil of Olay or Rodan + Fields?
>
> Does it matter if I went to grad school or no school?
>
> Does it matter if I serve my kids whole foods or Happy Meals?
>
> Does it matter if my teenager is promiscuous or virginal?
>
> Does it matter if I get married or stay single?
>
> Does it matter if I abstain or imbibe?
>
> Does it matter if I save or spend?
>
> Does it matter if I stay or leave?
>
> Does it matter if I love or hate?

Do my choices have any impact? Does my life have any lasting impact or meaning?

We are studying the Wisdom Books, biblical literature that helps us make sense of life in God's world under his authority, and we've come to the book of Ecclesiastes. Those of us who expect every part of the Bible to wrap things up neat and tidy hardly know what to do with this book. In fact, on the surface it can confuse us more than inform us, perhaps leaving us with more questions than we came with. So to grow in wisdom from our study of Ecclesiastes, we first need to see how it fits into the Wisdom Literature.

We've just finished Proverbs, which is line after poetic line about the way things work in the world. If you work hard, you get rewarded. If you're not nice to other people, they won't be nice to you. It can seem cut-and-dried and perfectly orderly. But anyone who lives in this world knows life does not always play by the rules. Certainly Job knew this. The orderliness of the universe was hidden to Job while his friends approached his problems with the dogmatic assumption that he was merely reaping what he sowed, just like the proverb said.

Similarly, Ecclesiastes argues against simplistic explanations for how things work in the world and rejects the suggestion that God's actions in the world are wholly predictable. Rather than God's ways being hidden, the words of this book suggest that God's ways are unknowable—that "he is active in the world, but so much of what he does is unexplained and beyond finding out."[1] In Ecclesiastes we hear the voice of someone who lives in a world of disappointment and confusion and cruelty, trying to figure out if anything really matters.

To grasp the wisdom God intends for us to gain from this enigmatic book of the Old Testament, we need first to get a sense of the big picture, because how we start to see this book shapes how we read the rest of it. It is important to recognize that there are really two voices speaking in this book. One is a sort of narrator. He introduces the book, and for the first eleven verses we hear him speaking, in a sense introducing the primary speaker in the book. Our narrator introduces him this way:

The words of the Preacher, the son of David, king in Jerusalem. (Eccles. 1:1)

The word translated "Preacher" is, literally, a convener, someone who assembles a group of people, presumably to teach or preach. Some assume this preacher is Solomon because he is identified as "the son of David, king in Jerusalem," and we know that Solomon was a son of David and was known for having wisdom. But there are some reasons we might not assume that this preacher is Solomon, as there are things the preacher tells about that don't reflect what we know about the golden era of Solomon's reign. The author may also simply be indicating continuity with the wisdom traditions of Solomon, not claiming identity, or perhaps creatively presenting his thought in the character of Solomon.

So there are reasons to think it is Solomon and reasons to think it isn't. But really, it doesn't matter. We will give him a name, calling him Qoheleth, which is the Hebrew word used throughout this book that is translated "the Preacher." Not exactly on the list of current top-ten baby names, but it will help us to remember that this is a unique person speaking throughout, telling us about his experiences, making observations, and asking questions.

At the end of the book, when the narrator speaks again to draw some conclusions from all that Qoheleth has said, he speaks to "my son." So we could imagine a scene in which a man is sitting with his son or protégé, seeking to talk to him about what life means and what really matters in life, and he tells his son all about Qoheleth's pursuits and questions and then, at the end, draws his own conclusions about all that Qoheleth has had to say.

And when we think of it that way, we realize that everything Qoheleth says throughout the twelve chapters of Ecclesiastes may be true and sound on its own, or it may not. Perhaps the narrator is not necessarily endorsing everything Qoheleth says but is using his words as a foil for his argument and explanation to the son.[2] And the truth is, biblical theologians see it both ways. Some insist that all that Qoheleth says is sound (which makes it difficult to deal with some of the things he says that certainly don't seem that way). And some theologians paint all that he says as quite misguided (which makes it difficult to deal with some of what he says that rings true).

Certainly Qoheleth had some wisdom and was able to see into the difficult realities of life in this world. He also has lots of questions about this world and this life. Perhaps they are questions you've had too. Let's work our way through some, though certainly not all of them, to see where they lead. (And, along the way, if you think I'm asking a lot of questions without giving any answers, then you are getting a feel for what it was like to live in Old Testament times, waiting for more revelation from God.)

Does Anything Last?

After a brief, poetic introduction, Qoheleth, the preacher, sets the tone and direction for the book:

> I applied my heart to seek and to search out by wisdom all that is done under heaven. It is an unhappy business that God has given to the children of man to be busy with. I have seen everything that is done under the sun, and behold, all is vanity and a striving after wind. (Eccles. 1:13–14)

Immediately we sense this experience is not going to be a real upper. He has seen everything "under the sun," meaning everything that is in this world and goes on in this life, from a limited earthly perspective. And his estimation of it is that "all is vanity." The word translated "vanity" is used elsewhere in the Old Testament to describe a mere breath, like when we puff out a burst of air. The only time we can even see our breath is on a cold night, and it is there for a second and then gone. We can't collect it. It's gone. By saying "all is vanity," Qoheleth is saying that everything about this life under the sun is fleeting. It has no real substance. He has "picked up life in his hands and turned it over and over to see it from every angle, and he has become convinced that our lives are futile—but not in the sense that they are not worth living. So much of life doesn't last."[3]

And to a certain degree, we would have to agree. Long ago, in the garden, Adam and Eve worked the land under the sun, and their lives were filled with significance. They were made to last, and work was fulfilling, not futile. But then they sinned. And everything changed. What was intended to bring pleasure—tending and filling the earth, meaningful work, and child bearing—was forever after reduced to exasperating toil and filled with pain. And it wasn't just humanity that was plunged into this futility. Paul writes that the entire "creation was subjected to futility" (Rom. 8:20).

Qoheleth has raised the question, Does anything last? And the conclusion he has come to is that nothing lasts; all is vanity. He has become aware and makes us aware of the need for someone or something to set the creation free from this futility. But Qoheleth cannot see any hope of that from his earthbound perspective. His conclusion is:

> What is crooked cannot be made straight, and what is lacking cannot be counted. (Eccles. 1:15)

He has no sense that anything that has been ruined can be reclaimed, that anything empty can be filled, that anything old can be made new.

Does Anything Satisfy?

When Qoheleth claims that "all is vanity," he speaks from experience, because he tried it all—money, pleasure, knowledge, and power—in search of an answer to the question of whether anything under the sun can really satisfy.

> I said in my heart, "Come now, I will test you with pleasure; enjoy yourself." But behold, this also was vanity. (Eccles. 2:1)

He pursued pleasure, becoming an experimental hedonist. In other words, he made his personal happiness his chief end in life. He said to himself, "You deserve a break today" and "Have it your way" and "Go for all the gusto you can get." He sought out entertainment and imbibed in fine wine, built himself a beautiful home and populated his bed with myriad sexual partners. Pleasure seemed to hold out the promise of fulfillment, but it didn't last. He ended up empty, unsatisfied.

Giving up wisdom and going for folly didn't satisfy either. Throwing himself into work got him nowhere. He discovered that while pleasure and enjoyment in one's work are good and come from the hand of God, they don't last, at least not here under the sun. Qoheleth's research showed that earthly things offer no lasting satisfaction. It can't be had. What is needed is something that truly and deeply and lastingly satisfies. But what?

Is Anyone in Control?

Next, Qoheleth turns poetic, speaking the words of Ecclesiastes that may be the most familiar, and perhaps the most misunderstood:

> For everything there is a season, and a time for every matter under heaven:
>> a time to be born, and a time to die;
>> a time to plant, and a time to pluck up what is planted;
>> a time to kill, and a time to heal;
>> a time to break down, and a time to build up;
>> a time to weep, and a time to laugh;
>> a time to mourn, and a time to dance. (Eccles. 3:1–4)

Qoheleth is not suggesting that there is a time when you should set about doing all these things and that your happiness depends on knowing when to do what. Rather, he's saying that God has appointed times when all these things will happen, whether we like it or not. This is not a lovely folk song that should set you at ease with whatever comes but rather a sobering dose of reality that calls you to submit to God's sovereignty over time and events. Qoheleth concludes:

> He has made everything beautiful in its time. Also, he has put eternity into man's heart, yet so that he cannot find out what God has done from the beginning to the end. (Eccles. 3:11)

The word translated "beautiful" there can also mean "suitable." And in Hebrew, the emphasis falls on the word "everything." So we might read this verse, "He's appointed a suitable time for *everything*."[4] Yet he has "put eternity in man's heart." But this does not mean, as we often pluck it out of this context and interpret it to mean, that man has an inner sense that we were made to live forever. Instead, Qoheleth is saying that we can try to learn from the past, and we can try to prepare for the future, but God has already determined the end from the beginning, and no one can find it out. So he says that the unknowns of eternity in our hearts simply serve to make us miserable.

Because his knowledge of the one who holds the future is limited, his fear and frustration are magnified. The only thing he knows to expect is that one day he is going to turn back into dust. And as we read what he has written, we wonder with him, Is there anyone in control, someone who has the power to put an end to war and death and weeping and mourning so that it will finally be time for nothing but life and healing and laughing and dancing?

Is There Any Comfort?

In chapter 4 the topic changes from the times God has set to the misery of oppression, envy, and loneliness.

> Again I saw all the oppressions that are done under the sun. And behold, the tears of the oppressed, and they had no one to comfort them! (Eccles. 4:1)

Qoheleth considers all of the oppression experienced by people who live under the sun, the way in which the powerful exploit the weak for their own advantage. He sees the need for a comforter for those who hurt, an advocate for those who have no voice, but he finds none.

Qoheleth wonders about the person who works and saves all his life and has no one to leave his riches to. What's the point?, he asks. What or who can relieve the misery caused by oppression, envy, and loneliness?

Does Anyone Dare Draw Near?

For four chapters Qoheleth has confined himself to observations, describing his frustration with the futility of life under the sun, chronicling his responses to that futility. But now, in chapter 5, he turns to offering an answer to this depressing situation. This is the first time he has spoken at all about a relationship with God. God has been an omnipotent power and judge, but now Qoheleth speaks of an actual two-way relationship:

> Guard your steps when you go to the house of God. To draw near to listen is better than to offer the sacrifice of fools, for they do not know that they are doing evil. Be not rash with your mouth, nor let your heart be hasty to utter a word before God, for God is in heaven and you are on earth. Therefore let your words be few. . . . When you vow a vow to God, do not delay paying it, for he has no pleasure in fools. Pay what you vow. . . . For when dreams increase and words grow many, there is vanity; but God is the one you must fear. (Eccles. 5:1–2, 4, 7)

Qoheleth urges Israel to worship God in his house with reverence, to draw near to listen, and to be slow to speak. He admonishes God's people to be careful about the vows they make to God and to follow through on commitments made to him, saying, "God is the one you must fear." We sense here an uneasy relationship with God, that God is not going to put up with any nonsense. There is no sense of genuine intimacy or satisfaction found even in this, however. Something more personal, someone more approachable, is needed.

Is Anything Gained?

In chapter 2 Qoheleth lamented the futility of building up wealth, only to leave it to someone after he dies, but now, in chapter 6, he explores the possibility that there is something to be gained in having wealth to enjoy in this life under the sun. Yet he recognizes that no matter how much money a person has, it never seems to be enough:

> All the toil of man is for his mouth, yet his appetite is not satisfied. (Eccles. 6:7)

And we know that he is onto something here because we see this in ourselves. We can't sleep for worrying about potential damage to our possessions or portfolio. We hoard wealth, hoping it will protect us, only to develop a health problem that money cannot solve. We think what we need is a new couch and then we'll be satisfied, but that new couch makes the carpet look soiled, so we can't be happy until it is replaced. We have multiple computers in our homes, and yet we want to be first in line to get the latest new gadget. Is this not futility? Is not the elusive nature of "enough" really chasing after wind?

What we need is a way to make a profit that can't be eaten away, a gain that is not vulnerable to loss, riches that will not bring ruin but will be our reward. But where can we find this kind of currency?

Is There Any Hope?

What good is fighting against all this futility, Qoheleth seems to ask:

> For who knows what is good for man while he lives the few days of his vain life, which he passes like a shadow? For who can tell man what will be after him under the sun? (Eccles. 6:12)

Qoheleth wonders if God even knows what is good for man, because it is not apparent from anything he can see under the sun that God pursues man's good. He finds himself in a terrible dilemma. If life under the sun is all there is, then death must be better than such meaningless futility. But he has no sense of knowing what awaits him beyond the doors of death once he is done with this life under the sun.

What he needs is a promise of hope beyond the grave from someone who can be trusted. But where will he find this hope, this assurance?

Does Anyone Know?

Qoheleth has sought after wisdom, and there are some things he has figured out as he has faced life and death squarely and soberly. But there are so many things he cannot figure out and so many things that he decides are simply beyond knowing. There are paradoxes that simply don't make sense to him. Bad things happen to some good people and good things to some bad people. The future is a mystery to him, and he laments that we can't know the future and are powerless to control the present. He cannot figure out how to make sense of the grave injustices in this world as he sees wicked people lauded for their greatness and righteous people forgotten and derided.

And so he is left with more questions than answers. What does the future hold? When will justice come?

Is This All There Is?

It seems to Qoheleth that being God's chosen people in covenant with him gets you zip, nada. You live and die in this world like everyone else. So he suggests:

> Go, eat your bread with joy, and drink your wine with a merry heart. . . . Enjoy
> life with the wife whom you love, all the days of your vain life that he has
> given you under the sun, because that is your portion in life. (Eccles. 9:7, 9)

Food, drink, and merriment is the best that can be hoped for under the sun, according to Qoheleth. Everyone is subject to time and chance, to death at the last, and to unexpected misery until then. From here in chapter 9 to chapter 12, Qoheleth's advice could be summed up with these maxims: *Enjoy life. Remember death. Use wisdom. Take risks.*

Remember your Creator. And then he ends the same way he began, seemingly having made no real progress at all:

> Vanity of vanities, says the Preacher; all is vanity. (Eccles. 12:8)

The sum of Qoheleth's message is that all is vanity, that nothing ultimately matters and nothing really lasts. But this isn't the end of the book. And this isn't necessarily the narrator's summation. In Ecclesiastes 12:9 the narrator who began the book speaks again. We can almost see him turning to his son to bring Qoheleth's lengthy rhetoric in for a landing.

> Besides being wise, the Preacher also taught the people knowledge, weighing and studying and arranging many proverbs with great care. The Preacher sought to find words of delight, and uprightly he wrote words of truth. (Eccles. 12:9–10)

First the narrator commends Qoheleth, saying that certainly he got some things right. He was good at seeing the superficiality and contradictions of life, but clearly he was bad at finding meaning and redemption. Though he wrote with clarity, artistry, and integrity, and his take on life lived under the sun often rings true, he was looking at life only as we see it from our place under the sun, not from God's perspective. If we look at only a slice of time and earthly reality and understanding and take a personal, just God out of the equation, life becomes unbearably pointless. The narrator goes on to say:

> The words of the wise are like goads, and like nails firmly fixed are the collected sayings; they are given by one Shepherd. (Eccles. 12:11)

A goad is one of the tools of a shepherd's trade, a sharp stick that spurs a stubborn beast to keep moving. Ecclesiastes does that for people of faith. Its words goad the conscience and stimulate the soul. It makes us think critically about our calling, our cravings, our consumption, our culture. Qoheleth's words prod us not to expect lasting satisfaction in the things this world keeps telling us will make us happy. When we forget about God, Qoheleth prods us to remember our Creator. And the moment we begin to think that we will live forever, he pokes us in the ribs and reminds us that soon we will die.

Next the narrator gives the son a direct warning:

> My son, beware of anything beyond these. Of making many books there is no end, and much study is a weariness of the flesh. (Eccles. 12:12)

These are the final words that wisdom has to offer. Qoheleth has written himself out of a job by showing the futility of wisdom sought under the sun. While Qoheleth has said many wise things, many things that are true about the world, his "wisdom can't take us any farther; and it doesn't take us far enough."[5]

> *What is needed is not more wisdom writing, but the embodiment of God's wisdom.*

What is needed is not more wisdom writing, but the embodiment of God's wisdom. What is needed is a new kind of revelation, one that will enter into this life under the sun and thereby transform it. What is needed is one who will be so wise and accomplish so many things in wisdom that "were every one of them to be written, . . . the world itself could not contain the books that would be written" (John 21:25). What is needed is wisdom that comes from heaven, not from under the sun.

Does Anything Matter?

At this point the narrator leans in and looks his son square in the eyes and states the conclusion that all twelve chapters of Ecclesiastes have been driving toward:

> The end of the matter; all has been heard. Fear God and keep his commandments, for this is the whole duty of man. For God will bring every deed into judgment, with every secret thing, whether good or evil. (Eccles. 12:13–14)

This is it. This very sound but limited conclusion is as far as Old Testament Wisdom Literature can take us. It's as far as the entirety of the Old Testament can take us. And it leaves us wanting. All of us who have not feared God but instead have been flippant about him, all of us who have rebelled and ignored his commandments rather than obeyed them, need a greater conclusion to come to. Ecclesiastes leaves us with a gap that needs to be filled, a problem that must be addressed, and so many questions that need to be answered that are answered only in the incarnation of God's wisdom, Jesus Christ. Let's think our way back through the questions raised by Qoheleth:

Does anything last? Yes it does. While all creation was subjected to futility, it was subjected to futility "in hope that the creation itself will be set free from its bondage to corruption and obtain the freedom of the glory of the children of God" (Rom. 8:20–21). Yes, this life sometimes seems futile, and we know that so much about life in this world is so broken and does not work. But we have hope that this futility will not be the way things are forever because Jesus has accomplished all that is necessary for creation to be set free from its futility.

Does anything satisfy? Yes. Jesus offers himself to all of those looking to find satisfaction in the pleasures that this world offers, saying, "Everyone who drinks of this water will be thirsty again, but whoever drinks of the water that I will give him will never be thirsty again. The water that I will give him will become in him a spring of water welling up to eternal life" (John 4:13–14).

Is anyone in control? Yes. Jesus is control. He "upholds the universe by the word of his power" (Heb. 1:3). While here, under the sun, there is a time for war and a time for death, a time for mourning and a time for tears, the day is coming when the time for these things will run out. Jesus will put an end to war and death and mourning and will "wipe away every tear" for all time (Rev. 21:4).

Is there any comfort? Yes. "We have an advocate with the Father, Jesus Christ the righteous" (1 John 2:1). Jesus is the one who has given us "eternal comfort and good hope through grace" (2 Thess. 2:16).

Does anyone dare draw near? Yes. Jesus has opened up the way to God by taking our sin, which has separated us from him, upon himself and by giving to us his own righteous merit. We have not kept our vows to God, but Jesus has as our substitute. You can "draw near to the throne of grace," not in fear of condemnation but in confidence that you will "receive mercy and find grace to help in time of need" (Heb. 4:16).

Is there any hope beyond the grave? There is no hope apart from Christ. "And if Christ has not been raised, then our preaching is in vain and your faith is in vain. . . . If in Christ we have hope in this life only, we are of all people most to be pitied. But in fact Christ has been raised from the dead, the firstfruits of those who have fallen asleep" (1 Cor. 15:14, 19–20). Jesus gives us a sure hope of glory beyond the grave.

Does anyone know if justice will ever be done? Yes, it will—by the innocent one who was oppressed and abused and mistreated. "When he was reviled, he did not revile in return; when he suffered, he did not threaten, but continued entrusting himself to him who judges justly" (1 Pet. 2:23). Revelation gives us a glimpse of that day when justice is finally done.

Is this life all there is? No, my friends, this life is not all there is. Jesus has promised, "In my Father's house are many rooms. If it were not so, would I have told you that I go to prepare a place for you? And if I go and prepare a place for you, I will come again and will take you to myself, that where I am you may be also" (John 14:2–3).

Does anything matter? Yes, it does. Qoheleth could not see the full picture when he assumed that man gains nothing by his toil under the sun. There is much to be gained, but we can't expect to get it here under the sun. Instead, Jesus said, "Your reward is great in heaven" (Luke 6:23). Because of Christ, you can "be steadfast, immovable, always abounding in the work of the Lord, knowing that in the Lord your labor is not in vain" (1 Cor. 15:58). Everything you've done in Christ, for Christ, and through Christ will matter forever. To live is Christ. It's not futile. And to die is gain (Phil. 1:21). With Christ, we'll live forever.

Looking Forward: The End of the Matter

Throughout Ecclesiastes, Qoheleth has asked again and again if there is more to life than what we can see and experience living under the sun. And the narrator wants us to know that there is:

> The end of the matter; all has been heard. Fear God and keep his commandments, for this is the whole duty of man. For God will bring every deed into judgment, with every secret thing, whether good or evil. (Eccles. 12:13–14)

Proverbs tells us that the fear of the Lord is "the beginning of wisdom." And from Ecclesiastes we learn that the fear of the Lord is also "the end of the matter." The fear of the Lord is not just the beginning but also the end; in fact, it is the essence of our entire existence.

The final message of Ecclesiastes is not that nothing really matters but that everything matters. If there is a God who will one day judge the world, then everything matters. God will bring *every* deed into judgment, including *every* secret thing. Nothing will be excluded. What we did, how we did it, and why we did it will all have eternal significance. And that is good news, isn't it? Doesn't it take away the sense of meaningless that we sometimes feel?

Well, yes, but if God is going to bring everything—good or evil—under judgment, what does that mean for those of us who have said and done many evil things that we know are worthy of condemnation? As we think it through, this does not, on the surface, seem like good news at all.

But then we remember that the conclusion of Ecclesiastes is not the whole story. We remember the gospel that it points us to with all of its unanswered questions. We hear the words of Jesus that the people in Qoheleth's day had not yet heard: "Truly, truly, I say to you, whoever hears my word and believes him who sent me has eternal life. He does not come into judgment, but has passed from death to life" (John 5:24).

Because we fear God and know him through his Son, Jesus Christ, rather than run from him in fear because we have not kept his commandments, we can run to him in fear and expect his acceptance. We can run to the foot of his cross and confess that we have not kept his commandments. We have thought of him flippantly rather than fearfully. And when we run to this one that we fear, rather than being condemned, we find mercy and grace.

After all our days of questing, at the end of our spiritual road we will arrive at the throne of eternal justice and meet the great Judge. When that day comes, it will be revealed that everything everyone ever did or said or thought has eternal significance—either confirming that our lives under the sun have been redeemed by the death of God's Son, or condemning us for lives lived in utter futility, always seeking but never finding, always grasping at the world's pleasures to find significance and satisfaction but never taking hold of Christ.

Soon Jesus will come again "on that day when, according to my gospel, God judges the secrets of men by Christ Jesus" (Rom. 2:16). But you do not have to live in fear of that day. The victory of Jesus will save you from the vanity of life under the sun. Your life will endure and not simply fade away, not because of your goodness but because of his grace.

'Twas grace that taught my heart to fear,
And grace my fears relieved.

Discussion Guide

Ecclesiastes

Getting the Discussion Going

1. What are some things about life in this world "under the sun" that are frustrating, unfulfilling, or don't last that the writer of Ecclesiastes also found to be empty or "vanity."

Getting to the Heart of It

2. In Ecclesiastes we are listening to a thinker who seems to be pulled by two perspectives: one based on the knowledge of God and the other based on his own experience and observations. How do these two perspectives seem to clash with one another throughout Ecclesiastes?

3. Look back at question 6 in the Personal Bible Study. What does the New Testament say about this life under the sun?

4. Does the New Testament affirm that "all is vanity"? To support your answer, share the insights you found in the verses you looked up in question 11.

5. The narrator gives the son a direct warning about something that is in vogue in our day, and that is to be forever on a spiritual search without ever finding, deciding, or embracing the truth. Many voices in our world today suggest that it is arrogant to claim to have found what is true and to put confidence in it. What would be the narrator's response to that, according to the final few verses of Ecclesiastes?

6. Ecclesiastes doesn't have any prophecies about or references to Christ unless, perhaps, we see Qoheleth's limited wisdom as pointing us to Jesus, the greater preacher of the meaning of life, or if we see him shadowed in the shepherd who give words of wisdom in Ecclesiastes 9:11. But, in a larger way, how would you explain to someone how the book of Ecclesiastes points us toward or prepares us for Christ?

Getting Personal

7. Qoheleth sought to find satisfaction in a number of things that did not ultimately satisfy. And he had a number of questions about the realities of this world that he could not find answers to. Which of his pursuits and perplexities could you especially relate to?

Getting How It Fits into the Big Picture

8. Throughout this study we have been considering how what we are studying fits into the larger story of God's plan of redemption and his written revelation. How does Ecclesiastes point back to what happened in the garden as well as to what is to come when Christ returns, according to Romans 8:20–23?

Song of Solomon

Song of Solomon

1. Take a few minutes to read the Song of Solomon. It might sound like a big assignment to read the whole book, but you will see that its eight chapters have only 117 verses. On this quick read-through, you're not looking for any answers or getting stuck trying to figure anything out. Your goal is to get a feel for the book and its flow, allowing it to raise questions in your mind that you hope to get answered. What are your general impressions about this book? What questions do you hope to get answered?

Song of Solomon has been read and interpreted in vastly different ways throughout the history of the church. So our goal in studying the Song of Solomon this week will not be to nail down the "correct" interpretation of this enigmatic book but rather to familiarize ourselves with it and with the various ways it can be read, and to enjoy it. Rather than becoming frustrated by the ways it does not fit into the mold of our modern Western thinking, we want to enter into its Near Eastern ancient context and let it speak to us, as the whole of the Bible speaks to us, about the goodness of God and his plan to redeem all things through Christ—including human love.

Having read through the book, you may have struggled to find a storyline. Perhaps it doesn't have one. You may have struggled to know who was saying what. That is not always particularly clear either. As we study Song of Solomon, we need to consider three important questions about the text, remembering that these questions have been and continue to be answered in differing ways by faithful Bible scholars and interpreters.

~ Is this written by Solomon, about Solomon, or perhaps simply written under Solomon's oversight during his lifetime?
~ What kind of literature are we reading?
~ Who are the characters we hear speaking?

Let's consider each question, understanding that our conclusion about each one impacts our conclusions about the other two. *Is this written by Solomon, about Solomon, or perhaps simply written under Solomon's oversight during his lifetime?* In the first verse we read:

> The Song of Songs, which is Solomon's. (Song 1:1)

This is grammatically ambiguous. It could mean that it was written by Solomon, or it could mean only that it was written in his honor. We know from 1 Kings 11 that Solomon was not exactly an expert in healthy sexual relationships. It tells us that he "loved many foreign women" (1 Kings 11:1). In fact, he had "700 wives, princesses, and 300 concubines" (v. 3), and "his wives turned away his heart after other gods, and his heart was not wholly true to the LORD his God" (v. 4). It could be that this book was written not by him or even about him (since he is mentioned only generally as a distant figure) but simply during his lifetime, or under his oversight, or perhaps to present to him. (Can you see already that we aren't going to be able to nail down all of our conclusions about this book?)

Why is it called the "Song of Songs"? To say it is "the best of songs" is to denote a superlative, similar to expressions such as "holy of holies" (as some translations render "Most Holy Place") and "King of kings and Lord of Lords." This is the love song that surpasses all other love songs.

What kind of literature are we reading? We recognize right away when we come to Song of Solomon that these are not songs like the psalms are songs. Neither is this narrative story like we read in the history books of the Bible. And it isn't propositional analytical teaching like the letter to the Romans. In fact, the Song of Solomon is a unique literary genre in the Old Testament.

Some read Song of Solomon as a *drama* that tells a story, either about two lovers—King Solomon and a shepherdess, or a shepherd and a shepherdess in ancient Israel—or about a love triangle between King Solomon, a shepherd, and shepherdess.

For much of history, Song of Solomon has been read as *allegory*. Jewish interpreters have read it is an allegory about God's relationship to his beloved Israel, and Christian interpreters have read it as an allegory about Christ's relationship to his bride, the church. Those who read the book this way would say that when the book begins with the bride's statement of desire, "Let him kiss me with the kisses of his mouth!" (Song 1:2), this expresses the believer's desire for fresh experiences of Christ's love. They would say that kisses represent the Word of God, that the woman's breasts represent the nurturing doctrine of the church, and that her lips represent law and gospel.

A good example of an allegory is *The Pilgrim's Progress* by John Bunyan. This story was written to describe a Christian's journey to heaven using the literary tool of allegory. Everything in the story represents something else, and it is clear to us as the reader that we are to read it this way. But the Song of Solomon does not make it clear that it is to be read as allegory. And, in fact, if we try to make the details in the book fit an allegorical reading, we have to make some strange interpretive leaps, especially when the imagery is especially erotic. So, those who oppose the view of reading this book as allegory would say that, in the Song of Solomon, kisses are kisses and breasts are breasts, and when the woman invites her beloved to come to her garden and eat its choicest fruits, she is inviting her husband to enjoy her body in sexual intimacy.

What seems to make the most sense to me is that Song of Solomon is *love poetry*. It is a collection of poems that celebrates sexual love. What is less clear is how or if the poems are connected to each other. Each of the songs may be about different characters and may even have different authors. But because we find repeated imagery, settings, themes, and characters, as well as a repeated refrain or chorus, it would seem to indicate a connection between the poems. This does not mean, however, that we can impose a linear storyline or sequence on the poems. To use a modern analogy, if we see Song of Solomon as a collection of unconnected poetry, we would need to read it not like a Shakespearean play (which has a plot) but like a collection of Shakespearean love poems.

But we can't ignore the fact that the book seems to have some story to it, even if it is not told in the linear way we modern readers like to read a story. So while we don't see a sequential storyline, perhaps we do see poetic structure. "Hebrew stories and poetry often follow what is called a 'chiastic' structure. This simply means that the work has a central pivot of meaning from which it moves outward symmetrically in both directions. The beginning and ending, then, will match, in a sense, as they are both farthest away from the middle."[1] So, if we were to diagram the Song, it might look like this:

A. Home in the country
B. Developing love
   C. Dream sequence
      D. Consummation
   C'. Dream sequence
B'. Developing love
A'. Home in the country

Seeing this structure at work in the Song of Solomon helps us to read it as a coherent series of love songs that intertwine, rather than as dramatic sequence that we try to force into a logical mold.[2]

Who are the characters we hear speaking? The Song of Solomon is a series of exchanges, mostly between two or three characters with chorus-like "Others" sprinkled in. These others usually pick up items from the lovers' speeches and urge the two forward in love.

If we want to understand the book, we must seek to identify who is speaking from verse to verse, as it is not indicated clearly in the text. If you read the Song in two or three different translations, you might find that the editors have identified the speakers differently. The variations of interpretation come from the fact that these headings are not indicated in the original text but have been created by translators and editors to aid readers in understanding.

There are three primary possible scenarios to explain who is speaking throughout Song of Solomon, each of which is based on differing understandings of the nature of the story.

In the first scenario, there are two characters, King Solomon and a young shepherdess. In this scenario King Solomon notices a chaste and attractive young vinedresser in one of his vineyards, falls in love with her, marries her, and brings her into his court. One version of this story sees the young bride as shy and reluctant to open the door to her husband, and another sees the bride as devoted but struggling with the polygamy of the king. In this storyline, the conclusion of the Song, "Set me as a seal upon your heart" (Song 8:6), is a call for her husband to be as exclusively dedicated to her as she is to him.

One problem with this storyline is that some elements of the story, e.g., his shepherding in the fields, make it difficult to identify the bridegroom as a king. Additionally, we know from 1 Kings (3:1; 7:8; 9:24; 11:1) that if there was a favored woman in Solomon's life, it was the Pharaoh's daughter, whom he married very early; it was not a working woman from the king's flocks and vineyards who is pictured in the Song. If this woman was one of the scores of Solomon's wives, it doesn't seem that the romance between them would have such deep sincerity. If it did, why would Solomon add hundreds more women to his harem?

In the second scenario there are three characters: King Solomon, a young shepherdess, and a shepherd. In this scenario, King Solomon falls in love with a young, virtuous shepherdess and brings her into his court, but she is really in love with a shepherd and apparently leaves Solomon for her shepherd lover in the country.

While this storyline helps to explain the references to the bridegroom as a king, it seems unlikely that Solomon would be treated as an interloper in a work that is dedicated to him. Also, there is no indication in the text that would differentiate definitively between the voices of Solomon and the shepherd.

In the third scenario, there are two characters, a shepherd and a shepherdess. In this scenario we are reading a series of exchanges mostly between two betrothed Israelites. These two peasants refer to each other in royal terms. The simple shepherd is as King Solomon in her eyes, and she is a princess in his. Sometimes the bride is speaking; other times we hear her thoughts and perhaps an account of her dreams.

Do all of these possibilities cause you some confusion or frustration? Most of us are more comfortable with reading things in which events are related in a sequential flow of time. But in Hebrew literature, such as the Song of Solomon, the sequence of events is not necessarily time-ordered. In addition, many of us are used to reading the Bible with left-brain rationalism rather than right-brain artistry. Song of Solomon, as poetry, is meant to spark our imagination, stir our emotions, and awaken all of our senses. Don't let the enigmas of this book rob you of its joy and beauty.

Now that you are more familiar with the possible scenarios and characters, read through Song of Solomon again, imagining that you are listening to a reader's theatre. Seek to determine the backdrop for each section as well as who is speaking. Enjoy its vivid and tactile imagery, its flowery and fruitful landscape, and its romance and wonder, and seek to understand its poetic allusions. Don't worry about a time sequence; let each section be what it is. And look for key themes, repeated phrases, and images.

2. A refrain repeated throughout the book is found in Song 2:7; 3:5; and 8:4. While the speaker is uncertain, the tone is commanding. Who is being spoken to, and how would you paraphrase what is being said in this repeated refrain?

3. Why do you think this refrain is repeated throughout this book of love poetry?

4. A key passage in the Song is found in 8:6–7. What do you think the speaker is asking for, and what is she saying about the nature of love?

While we would not suggest that Song of Solomon is an allegory, in which every image of the story represents something else, we do know that the marriage relationship is used as a vehicle to illustrate spiritual realities throughout Scripture. So while the Song is primarily a celebration of love and the gift of sexual intimacy, we cannot help but hear echoes of the passionate love Christ has for his bride and feel a longing for our complete oneness with him to be consummated when he returns for us, his bride.

5. Read the following passages, which use the human marriage relationship as a vehicle to illustrate spiritual realities. Beside each reference note a particular phrase in the passage that is most meaningful to you.

~ Isaiah 54:5–8

~ Isaiah 62:5

~ Hosea 2:16–20

~ Ephesians 5:22–32

~ Revelation 19:6–9

Teaching Chapter

Kiss Me

I'm sure the really spiritual girls were doing really spiritual things after the Youth for Christ rallies I went to on Saturday nights when I was in the eighth grade. Me? I was outside in the parking lot kissing Bobby Taggart.

Like most of you, I was on a search for that special someone who was witty and wonderful and worthy of having his name added to mine in the eternal equation of love: Nancy + _____ = LOVE FOREVER. I was looking for someone who would help me to answer the question we all have deep inside: Am I lovable? Is there anyone out there who will be interested in knowing the real me, and, once he does, will he still love me the way I long to be loved?

We women usually have someone in mind who is at least as cute as and hopefully taller than Tom Cruise, who will show up at our door, look at us across the room, and say, as he fights back tears, "You complete me."

But could there ever be a human being who could satisfy our cavernous needs and desires? Is the pleasure of a human kiss the ultimate experience? Or is it possible that our sexual desires could be pointing us toward something far deeper, something far longer lasting?

We've been working our way through the Old Testament's Wisdom Books, looking at how a wise person living under God's authority suffers, how he praises his God, and how she laments her difficult circumstances. We've seen how a person who fears the Lord chooses a pathway to pursue. Last week we saw how a person who lives life under the sun instead of under God's rule finds emptiness, while a person whose life is united to Christ finds meaning and purpose. This week, as we turn to the Song of Solomon, we discover how a wise person living in covenant with his or her Creator enjoys God's good gift of sexual desire.

And it is kind of shocking to just say it, right? We feel a little awkward talking about sex—especially in church. Some of us think of sex as dirty, so discussing it seems unseemly. Some of us think of sex as private, so it seems inappropriate. And some of us are filled with shame when the topic of sex is raised, and it makes us uncomfortable.

But interestingly the Bible does not find sex awkward or something to be ashamed of. At the very beginning of the Bible, when God made a woman from the rib he had taken from the man and brought her to the man, the man broke out into the world's first love poem:

> This at last is bone of my bones
> > and flesh of my flesh;
> she shall be called Woman,
> > because she was taken out of Man. (Gen. 2:23)

Moses then adds this commentary, helping us to see that God celebrates the goodness of sexual love:

> Therefore a man shall leave his father and his mother and hold fast to his wife, and they shall become one flesh. And the man and his wife were both naked and were not ashamed. (Gen. 2:24–25)

They were naked and unashamed, living together and loving each other in a beautiful garden with complete freedom. The intertwining of their lives and bodies was so intimate that it can be described only as becoming "one flesh." There was no self-centeredness to come between Adam and Eve, no shame to make them self-conscience. At least not yet.

But when Adam and Eve sinned, it not only interrupted their intimacy with God; it alienated them from each other. They went from being naked and unashamed to trying to cover up their shame and nakedness with fig leaves. Their relationship, which had been only open and pure and enjoyable, now became marked by manipulation and conflict and disappointment.

And we have inherited this sin-affected, shame-infected sexuality from our first parents, Adam and Eve. While there is still so much to the one-flesh union God gave that is so good, the reality is that we all express our sexuality in broken ways because we are all sinners. This brokenness is evidenced in some of us as sexual obsession; for others, sexual aversion; and for still others, sexual perversion. Some struggle with same-sex attraction and others with a repressed sexual appetite. Some have been sexually abused, and some have been abusers. Some of us have used sex as a weapon by withholding it, while others have made it an idol as we've indulged in it—even if only in our imaginations.

Sex is such an uncomfortable topic that we're a bit surprised to find a whole book in the Bible about sexual love, aren't we? So why is this book in the Bible? What is it that God wants us to see about sexual love in its 117 verses? And if the whole Bible is really about Christ, as Jesus said it is, how does Song of Solomon uniquely reveal Christ to us, when it never even mentions God?[3]

It is always good to begin trying to understand a book of the Bible by determining what kind of literature we are reading. So what kind of literature are we reading when we read Song of Solomon? The truth is, no book in the Bible has had a greater diversity in terms of how people interpret it, and so we must come to the text with humility. Is this historical—the story of a real couple? Is this a drama about an imaginary couple? Is it an allegory in which the characters and everything else are all intended to represent something or someone else?

The challenge with reading Song of Solomon as a drama or story is that there is no narrator guiding us in how to identify the main characters and follow the storyline, and in fact there are many different possible storylines. It would seem that reading it as a story of real people or imagined characters would force us to impose a storyline on the book that isn't really there. This makes reading and understanding this book difficult for us as modern readers, because we want to find a sequence of events in the book and consistency of characters, and we don't.

For much of history, Song of Solomon has been read as allegory, perhaps prompted more by discomfort with its sexual content than with evidence in the text. Jewish readers read it as an allegory about

God's love relationship to Israel. And certainly we know that Scripture often describes God as a lover who is jealous for the exclusive affections of adulterous Israel. Until the 1800s most Christian interpreters read Song of Solomon as an extended allegory about Christ and his bride, the church. And once again, we know that Scripture is replete with language of Christ's love for his church. Certainly there are some messages here for us about the intensity of Christ's love for his bride, about the desire he has for us, and the pleasure he takes in us. But to recognize some larger messages as pointers to Christ does not require that we read the book as an allegory in which kisses aren't kisses but stand for something else, something spiritual. To read Song of Solomon as an allegory requires some real gymnastics when we come to its very erotic passages. While the book seems to point thematically to Christ's loving intentions for his bride, if we try to force the verse-by-verse detail of Song of Solomon to fit an allegorical reading of the book, we have to make some fanciful and awkward leaps.

So if this book isn't a drama and it isn't an allegory, what is it? There is some agreement among interpreters today that this book is a collection or anthology of love poems that does not so much chronicle a story as evoke a mood. Some would count as many as twenty love poems bound together with some consistency of characters, refrains, and repeated images. And some would say that the consistencies that bind the poems together indicate that there is at least some structure to it.

We can explore Song of Solomon as if we are walking through an exhibition at an art gallery of the work of one artist. All of the paintings have a similar style and some of the same subjects. And "as we move from one picture to the next, we recognize many of the same underlying patterns while noting the subtle changes in details."[4] But rather than read it seeking to make verse-by-verse application, we must listen for its larger messages.

Song of Solomon seems to be a cycle of poetry about two lovers set in a flowery and fruitful rural landscape. This love poetry is unapologetically sexual as it depicts marital love. And while it is very erotic, it isn't at all bawdy or vulgar.

There is an important distinction between what is erotic and what is pornographic. The erotic and pornographic are both concerned with sex, but while the erotic approaches sex obliquely and with restraint, the pornographic approaches sex directly and with no restraint. While the erotic has depth and dimension and approaches people as subjects in relationships, the pornographic is shallow and designed for immediate sexual gratification and is concerned with people only as objects of sexual stimulation.[5]

Sometimes we're so fearful of slipping into the pornographic that we are uncomfortable with any depiction of sexuality. But clearly we learn from the outset of Song of Solomon that sex is not inherently dirty or shameful. In fact, the picture of sexuality painted by the writer of the Song harkens back to the garden of Eden, where Adam and Eve enjoyed the beautiful wonder of being naked and unashamed. It begins:

> Let him kiss me with the kisses of his mouth!
> For your love is better than wine;
>   your anointing oils are fragrant;
> your name is oil poured out;
>   therefore virgins love you.
> Draw me after you; let us run.
>   The king has brought me into his chambers. (Song 1:2–4)

This book opens with the young woman expressing her deepest feelings. She wants to be kissed by her lover, and not just a peck on the cheek. She wants to feel his mouth pressed deep inside her own. She wants him to pull her close and take her away to his chambers, where they can be alone.

Some who read Song of Solomon become nervous because it can appear that the sexual relationship of these two lovers is consummated before they are married. But that imposes a sequential storyline on the book, and we have to remember that these are betrothed lovers and that betrothal in the ancient world was very different from our modern concept of engagement. Their relationship was irrevocably sealed. This is no modern romance novel portraying out-of-control passions or a casual hook-up, but a series of poems extolling the passion of married love.

Song of Solomon is a refreshingly realistic and unembarrassed ode to human sexuality. It's not a how-to manual, nor is it a moral treatise. If we dive into this book seeking to apply it verse-by-verse as a handbook for dating and marriage, it breaks down. It is a poetic celebration of sexual love within the commitment of marriage that includes a clear and repeated warning about the power of sexual desire and the danger of sexual relationship outside the safety of lifelong commitment. As we read and discuss Song of Solomon, we realize that sexual love as it was intended is not a taboo subject for polite company but is actually cause for public celebration.

> *Song of Solomon is a refreshingly realistic and unembarrassed ode to human sexuality.*

Over the course of eight chapters, we, the readers, get to see into the relationship between the two lovers so that we see the agonies as well as the ecstasies of a growing relationship: the pain of separation; the fears of loss; the obstacles and threats to love; and the cycle of anticipation, invitation, consummation, and appreciation, which are part of a real relationship over the long haul.

We know that all of Scripture is "breathed out by God and profitable for teaching, for reproof, for correction, and for training in righteousness" (2 Tim. 3:16). So as we read this divinely inspired love poetry, we need to ask the question, What is to be learned or taken away from this unique book of the Bible? What is the wisdom God wants to impart to us about how to live in this world wisely as sexual people? And since we know that Jesus pointed to the Old Testament in its entirety and said, "It is they that bear witness about me" (John 5:39), we also need to ask the question, In what way does Song of Solomon bear witness to Jesus Christ?

And God Said, "It Is Good."

Certainly one key message of this unique book of the Bible is that the sexual relationship between a man and a woman committed to each other for life is beautiful and good. "The Song presents sexuality as a good thing protected by marriage and not as an evil thing made permissible by marriage."[6] Most of the world sees Christians as very prudish or repressive about sex. But, in fact, sex is a God-invented way to say to another person, "I belong completely and exclusively and permanently to you." Sex creates deep intimacy, oneness, and communion between two people. "Human emotions come and go, and that there needs to be something binding to provide consistency and endurance. So God requires a binding, public, legal covenant as the infrastructure for intimacy."[7] And just as the covenant of marriage is necessary to safeguard the sexual relationship, so is the sexual relationship necessary for keeping the covenant of marriage. Sex revisits and reenacts that oneness that we have pledged to one another.

In the Song there is no implied admonition to ignore the outer appearance and to focus only on the other's intellect or character. These two lovers take great pleasure in each other's bodies, offering an inventory of delight as they feast their eyes on each other. Did you notice as you read through Song of Solomon this week that it is the woman who has the dominant voice throughout the poems? She is the one who seeks, pursues, initiates, and boldly exclaims her physical attraction (Song 5:10–16), and there is no shame in it.

And did you notice that Song of Solomon celebrates the joys of sexual love in marriage without any mention of children? This is amazing when we consider that it was written in an ancient Near Eastern context, a culture in which children were so important to a person's identity and legacy. Don't let anyone take the purpose of pleasure away from your understanding of God-given, God-blessed sexuality. Sex is not solely about procreation but also about pleasure—pleasure that is a gift from God. It is also clear that there are appropriate restraints or boundaries for enjoying this pleasure. In this book that celebrates sexuality, we find a wonderful paradox in a chorus that is repeated two more times and unifies the book:

> I adjure you, O daughters of Jerusalem,
>   by the gazelles or the does of the field,
> that you not stir up or awaken love
>   until it pleases. (Song 2:7; repeated in 3:5 and 8:4)

"Here is the shocking message for our culture: sexual desire can lie dormant. You can be a complete human being and not be having sex."[8] Your identity is not bound up in your sexual activity or lack thereof. You were made in the image of God, and you are being remade in the image of Christ. You find your identity in him.

Sex Is Powerful, Even Dangerous

Why is it that we should not "stir up or awaken love" before its proper time? That leads us to the second significant message of Song of Solomon: sexual desire is powerful—and even dangerous. We see this in the one place in the whole book where we are given a commentary on the nature of sexual love.

> Set me as a seal upon your heart,
>   as a seal upon your arm,
> for love is strong as death,
>   jealousy is fierce as the grave.
> Its flashes are flashes of fire,
>   the very flame of the LORD.
> Many waters cannot quench love,
>   neither can floods drown it.
> If a man offered for love
>   all the wealth of his house,
>   he would be utterly despised. (Song 8:6–7)

The woman asks her lover to place her as a seal over his heart—a seal signifying that she belongs to him, body and soul. She is saying, "Let's be exclusive and not let anyone else into this relationship." This is an image of total commitment that serves as protection.

She also portrays love that is "strong as death," jealousy that is "fierce as the grave. Its flashes are flashes of fire." Sexual love has the power to seal and the strength to kill. It is a fire that heals but can also scorch. Sexual union puts a "death grip" on us that is inescapable. You can't simply wash away the bonds of love. Sexual love is not something cheap and insignificant but something costly and substantial.

The power of love to both seal and singe is why the refrain throughout the book warns not to "stir up or awaken love until it pleases." And this is why God loves you enough to insist that you enjoy this kind of intimacy inside the safety of the bonds of marriage and not outside of it.

Top-forty radio can make love seem so sentimental, so simple, so safe. Sitcoms make casual sex seem so inconsequential and unfettered. But the lover in Song of Solomon knows that love is far more intense than mere sentimentalism, far more complex than mere words, far more dangerous than hurt feelings. Misuse or misdirect sexual desire and it has the power to inflict severe damage. The only way to safely maintain something with so much power is to experience it in a secure relationship sealed through lifelong commitment.

Sex is never just sex. It arouses intense jealousy. It imprints us deep in our souls. Everyone to whom we join ourselves, everyone we sleep with, pulls away taking a piece of us that we can never fully get back.

To play around with sexual intimacy outside of marriage is to play with fire. Perhaps you know this well because you have already been burned. Sexual images and memories are seared in your imagination, and you so wish you could wipe them away. If that is you, let the good news of the gospel be a balm that brings healing to your scars.

> *Jesus did not come to join himself to people perfect sexual histories, as if there is such a person. Jesus came for sick people—people who have been burned by sexual sin.*

The religious leaders of Jesus's day were offended when they found Jesus eating with immoral and sexually broken people. But Jesus said, "Those who are well have no need of a physician, but those who are sick. I have not come to call the righteous but sinners to repentance" (Luke 5:31–32). Jesus did not come to join himself to people who have perfect sexual histories, as if there is such a person. Jesus came for sick people—people who have been burned by sexual sin. He does not turn his back on sin-scarred people, even if those wounds were self-inflicted.

> But he was wounded for our transgressions;
>   he was crushed for our iniquities;
> upon him was the chastisement that brought us peace,
>   and with his stripes we are healed.

> All we like sheep have gone astray;
>> we have turned—every one—to his own way;
> and the LORD has laid on him
>> the iniquity of us all. (Isa. 53:5–6)

If you have been burned by the misuse of sex, fall into the arms of the lover of your soul. He will bring healing to hidden places of your sin-sick soul.

Even the Best Sex Leaves Us with a Longing

The third big message we take away from Song of Solomon is that even the best sexual relationship leaves us with an unsatisfied longing.

Now you're wondering where I get this, because it seems like there's a lot of pleasure and satisfaction in this love poetry. And there is. And like every really good love story, we want the Song of Solomon to end with "And they lived happily ever after." Yet when we come to the last two verses of the Song, we find that our young woman still has a longing. She wants to hear her lover's voice again. She wants him to come to her again:

> Make haste, my beloved,
>> and be like a gazelle
> or a young stag
>> on the mountains of spices. (Song 8:14)

Her lover has been with her, and they have experienced the best that sexual love has to offer, and while it was satisfying, she finds herself in a state of longing once again. She wants to hear his voice again, to be close to him again. Sexual love between husband and wife is a glorious cycle of desire, anticipation, consummation, and satisfaction that gives way to longing once again. Human sexual love, no matter how satisfying in the moment, provides no final, lasting satisfaction.

And if this is true in a good, stable, sexually satisfying marriage relationship, how much more true is it in a nonmarried sexual relationship that has no promise of ongoing commitment to meet each other's needs? How many people spend their lives searching for the perfect sexual partner and sexual experience only to find that that person never shows up, or does not stay?

Our unsatisfied sexual appetite tells us that we were made for a longer lasting satisfaction, a greater intimacy. "Sexual desire points us toward something eternally satisfying, something that is available to those who never have sex over the course of their lifetime."[9]

My friend, whether you are single or married, sexually satisfied or sexually frustrated, sexually hopeful or sexually defeated, would you allow this song above all other songs to point you toward the beauty of sexual love inside the bonds of marriage and more significantly toward the lover of your soul, Jesus Christ? If we look at the big-picture message of the book of Song of Solomon—at the joy of sexual oneness in marriage—we see the physical expression of a spiritual reality.

Throughout the Bible we find that marriage is a metaphor for God's relationship to his people. It is not that God looked at a human invention of marriage and decided that it would provide a good illustration he could use to communicate the relationship he intends to have with his people. Instead, we must realize, God created marriage between a man and a woman with this very purpose in mind.

Marriage is not primarily about finding the love of your life who will make you happy. And the Bible's instructions about marriage are not provided primarily to ensure your personal fulfillment. If you are married, the reason you are married is so that you can put the covenant-keeping love of Christ for his church on display for the world to see. This infuses our ordinary marriages with sacred meaning and purpose. Your marriage is meant to tell the truth about the gospel—that Christ died for his church that loves him, and he will never break covenant with his bride. And whether you are married or single, you say something equally significant about Christ's relationship to his people when you refuse to have sex with someone you are not married to. You say that Christ's relationship with his people is an exclusive, passionate relationship of self-giving.

That this is God's intention for marriage is spelled out for us in the New Testament where Paul quotes from Moses's account of the very first marriage and sexual union of Adam and Eve and says that it has always been most profoundly about Christ and the church:

> "Therefore a man shall leave his father and mother and hold fast to his wife, and the two shall become one flesh." This mystery is profound, and I am saying that it refers to Christ and the church. (Eph. 5:31–32)

The sexual union of husband and wife is a shadow or picture of Christ's relationship with his people. Christ's love for his church is passionate and personal and costly. In the cross of Jesus Christ we see a love that is as strong as death, jealousy to have us that is fierce as the grave. We see love that plunged Jesus into the burning flames of God's wrath so that we might not be scorched by its fire. Many waters cannot quench Christ's love, and neither can floods drown it. His love for us cannot be bought, but it is given to us at great cost.

> For I am sure that neither death nor life, nor angels nor rulers, nor things present nor things to come, nor powers, nor height nor depth, nor anything else in all creation, will be able to separate us from the love of God in Christ Jesus our Lord. (Rom. 8:38–39)

The most zealous commitment shared by the world's most committed lovers is merely a dim picture of Christ's commitment to love us. And while our vast longings to be loved will never be perfectly satisfied as long as we live in this broken world, one day all of our deepest longings will be satisfied fully and forever. At the marriage supper of the Lamb, we, along with all those who have been wooed by the dying love of our Bridegroom and cleansed by his blood, will be presented to him in purity and beauty. And concerning our longings for our Bridegroom to come, "he who testifies to these things says, 'Surely I am coming soon'" (Rev. 22:20).

So what do you think? Is the human kiss of a meant-to-be soulmate the ultimate experience, the most we can hope for? Or is a human kiss really only a living metaphor for the ultimate kiss?[10]

> Here is love, vast as the ocean, lovingkindness as the flood,
> When the Prince of Life, our Ransom, shed for us his precious blood.

On the mount of crucifixion fountains opened deep and wide;
Through the floodgates of God's mercy flowed a vast and gracious tide.
Grace and love, like mighty rivers, poured incessant from above,
And heaven's peace and perfect justice kissed a guilty world in love.[11]

Ultimate and lasting satisfaction is not found in the most delicious of human kisses. How many times do we have to go to bed with someone whose breath smells like apples (Song 7:8) and wake up to morning's stench to learn this lesson? We find our ultimate and lasting satisfaction not in the best human lover but in divine redeeming love poured out on guilty sinners. The kiss that will satisfy us into eternity is the kiss of God in Jesus Christ, the crucified Lord. This is the kiss that heals and makes whole.

Looking Forward: Prepared as a Bride Adorned for Her Husband

In Matthew 22 we read about an interaction between Jesus and the Sadducees, who ask Jesus a complicated question about whom a woman will be married to in the resurrection. Jesus answered them in a "you don't understand enough to even be asking the right question" kind of response:

> You are wrong, because you know neither the Scriptures nor the power of God. For in the resurrection they neither marry nor are given in marriage, but are like angels in heaven. (Matt. 22:29–30)

There is a part of us that feels sad when we read that, especially those of us who long to be reunited with a spouse who has gone ahead into the presence of God. But this verse is not taking away the joy of that reunion with those we love. God is not going to take away one of the supreme joys of life this side of heaven by putting an end to marriage. Rather than withdraw it, he will complete it. All that marriage is meant to point to today will be complete in the new heaven and the new earth. The need for marriage to point us toward the intimacy and consummation to come will have fallen away. Rather than being married or single individuals, we will, as the bride of Christ, the church, be united to our bridegroom, Jesus. That one marriage—our marriage to Christ—will be so completely satisfying that even the most wonderful earthly marriage couldn't be as fulfilling.

We will finally live in the complete joy we were meant for all along, enjoying the complete satisfaction we were always longing for. We'll have a perfect husband and enjoy a perfect marriage. All of the longings and desires of our hearts will be satisfied as Jesus, our bridegroom, takes us as his own bride.

> And I saw the holy city, new Jerusalem, coming down out of heaven from God, prepared as a bride adorned for her husband. And I heard a loud voice from the throne saying, "Behold, the dwelling place of God is with man. He will dwell with them, and they will be his people, and God himself will be with them as their God. (Rev. 21:2–3)

All of the longing to be together, all of our desire to be intimate, will finally be satisfied. For all eternity we'll gaze into the face of our Beloved and admire his beautiful perfections. No more relating to God from a distance, no more estrangement from him because of our sin. In this new intimacy we will enjoy the full meaning of Paul's words: "For now we see in a mirror dimly, but then face to face. Now I know in part; then I shall know fully, even as I have been fully known" (1 Cor. 13:12).

Today, the prospect of being fully known might bring fear because there is so much we would not want our beloved Bridegroom to see. But when the old order is passed way, along with it goes our old way of life—our old hypocrisies, our old hidden thoughts, our old issues. We'll have not only new bodies but new minds that are not plagued with cynicism or selfishness. We'll have new hearts that will not be vulnerable to lust or pride. We will not fear being completely known, because we'll have nothing to hide. God's work of sanctification will be complete so that we'll be purified through and through. On that day we'll be back in the garden with our groom; we'll be naked and unashamed.

Discussion Guide

Song of Solomon

Getting the Discussion Going

1. Can you remember the first movie you saw that profoundly moved you, shaped you, or perhaps scared you about the power of romantic love and sex?

Getting to the Heart of It

2. If we were to get our view of sex only from movies and television (including the commercials), what would that message be?

3. If we were to get our view of sex only from the sermons and teaching we've heard in church over the course of our lives, what would that message be?

4. If we were to get our view of sex only from the Bible, what would that message be?

5. As you read through Song of Solomon and asked yourself the three questions in the Personal Bible Study—Who wrote this book? What kind of literature am I reading? Who are the characters speaking?—what were your conclusions and why?

6. To interpret the Bible correctly, we have to think first about the author's intention for the original audience. What do you think the writer of Song of Solomon wanted to communicate to his original readers, the kingdom of Israel living under Solomon's rule?

7. If sex in marriage is a physical sign that points to a spiritual reality, to what spiritual reality does sex outside of marriage point?

8. In light of what we've read in Song of Solomon, do you think a sexless marriage might betray God's purpose for marriage as much as adultery?

9. What do Song of Solomon and the gospel it points to have to say to our current culture of hooking-up, recreational sex, friends with benefits, and serial monogamy?

Getting Personal

10. In the Song of Solomon, words of praise extolling the virtues of the bride's beloved flow freely and abundantly from the bride's lips, an overflow of her thoughts about and passion for him. As a member of the bride of Christ, what would you want to tell us about your beloved?

Getting How It Fits into the Big Picture

11. Throughout this study, we have sought to grasp how the passage we're studying fits into the bigger story of God's plan for redemption. To what future hope does Song of Solomon point us?

Bibliography

Books and Articles

Alcorn, Randy C. *Heaven*. Carol Stream, IL: Tyndale, 2004.

Baldwin, Bill. "This Meaningless Life." Series of unpublished notes on Ecclesiastes. http://bettercovenant.wordpress.com/2009/04/13/ecclesiastes/.

Belcher, Richard Paul. *The Messiah and the Psalms: Preaching Christ from All the Psalms*. Fearn, Ross-shire: Mentor, 2006.

Boice, James Montgomery. *Psalms 42–106*. Grand Rapids, MI: Baker, 1996.

Calvin, Jean, and James Anderson. *Commentary on the Book of Psalms*. Grand Rapids, MI: Baker, 2009.

Carson, D. A. *The Cross and Christian Ministry: Leadership Lessons from 1 Corinthians*. Grand Rapids, MI: Baker, 2004.

Chester, Tim. "On Answering a Fool: Making Sense of the Book of Proverbs" http://beginningwithmoses.org.

Clowney, Edmund D. "The Singing Savior." *Moody Monthly*, July-August, 1979.

Dever, Mark. *The Message of the Old Testament: Promises Made*. Wheaton, IL: Crossway, 2006.

ESV Study Bible, English Standard Version. Wheaton, IL: Crossway, 2008.

Fee, Gordon D., and Douglas K. Stuart. *How to Read the Bible for All Its Worth*. Grand Rapids, MI: Zondervan, 2003.

Futato, Mark David. *Transformed by Praise: The Purpose and Message of the Psalms*. Phillipsburg, NJ: P&R, 2002.

Gledhill, Tom. *The Message of the Song of Songs: The Lyrics of Love*. Leicester: Inter-Varsity, 1994.

Goldsworthy, Graeme. *Gospel and Wisdom*. In *The Goldsworthy Trilogy*. Exeter: Paternoster, 2000.

Greidanus, Sidney. *Preaching Christ from Ecclesiastes: Foundations for Expository Sermons*. Grand Rapids, MI: Eerdmans, 2010.

Guthrie, Nancy. *The One Year Book of Discovering Jesus in the Old Testament*. Carol Stream, IL: Tyndale, 2010.

Jackson, David R. *Crying Out for Vindication: The Gospel According to Job*. Phillipsburg, NJ: P&R, 2007.

Kaiser, Walter C. *The Messiah in the Old Testament*. Grand Rapids, MI: Zondervan, 1995.

Keller, Timothy J. "The Gospel and Sex." *Redeemercitytocity.com*, 2005.

Kidner, Derek. *Psalms: An Introduction and Commentary on Books I and II of the Psalms*. London: Inter-Varsity, 1995.

_____. *The Wisdom of Proverbs, Job, and Ecclesiastes: an Introduction to Wisdom Literature*. Downers Grove, IL: InterVarsity, 1985.

Longman, Tremper. *How to Read Proverbs*. Downers Grove, IL: IVP Academic, 2006.

_____. *How to Read the Psalms*. Downers Grove, IL: InterVarsity, 2005.

Lucas, Dick. "A Great Need." Sermon, n.d. http://www.proctrust.org.uk.

Mason, Mike. *The Gospel according to Job*. Wheaton, IL: Crossway, 2002.

Nielson, Kathleen Buswell. *Ecclesiastes and Song of Songs: Wisdom's Searching and Finding*. Phillipsburg, NJ: P&R, 2009.

Ryken, Philip Graham, and R. Kent Hughes. *Ecclesiastes: Why Everything Matters*. Wheaton, IL: Crossway, 2010.

Sanlon, Peter. "Knowing Wisdom, Knowing Jesus." http://beginningwith moses.org/bt-briefings/169/knowing-wisdom-knowing-jesus.

Sklar, Jay. *Psalms and Wisdom Notes*. Covenant Theological Seminary, Fall 2009.

Tidball, Derek. "Songs of the Crucified One: The Psalms and the Crucifixion." *Southern Baptist Journal of Theology*, Summer 2007, 52.

Wright, Christopher H. *Knowing Jesus through the Old Testament*. Downers Grove, IL: InterVarsity, 1995.

Audio

Ash, Christopher. "Jesus the Wisdom of God." Address given at All Saints, Little Shelford, Cambridge, February 21, 1999.

Clowney, Edmund P. "Preaching Christ from Psalms." A nine-part audio series given at Westminster Seminary, Escondido, CA, 1991.

Clowney, Edmund P., and Timothy J. Keller. "Preaching Christ in a Postmodern World." Audio recording. Reformed Theological Seminary, Jackson, MS, n.d.

Dennis, Jon. "Psalm 51" "Job-Song of Songs." Sermon, Holy Trinity Church, Chicago, IL, February 21, 2010.

DeYoung, Kevin. "The End of the Matter." Sermon, University Reformed Church, Lansing, MI, November 9, 2008.

_____. "Welcome to College: It's Nothing but Vanity." Sermon, University Reformed Church, Lansing, MI, August 24, 2008.

Ferguson, Sinclair B. "Divine Sufferer." Sermon, Park Cities Presbyterian Church, Dallas, TX, November 17, 2004.

_____. "Job—Between Heaven and Hell." Sermon, First Presbyterian Church, Colombia, SC, January 6, 2010.

_____. "Mining Wisdom from Proverbs." Sermon, First Presbyterian Church, Colombia, SC, January 12, 2011.

_____. "Our Emotions and Our Spirituality." http://thegospelcoalition. org/resources/a/our_emotions_and_our_spirituality.

Futato, Mark. "Psalms: Experiencing Kingdom Blessings." http://thegospel-coalition.org/resources/a/experiencing_kingdom_blessings.

_____. "Psalms: Living Under the King's Reign." http://004db15.netsol-host.com/sermons/archive/TheoCons/1150_1994TC03.mp3.

Goligher, Liam. "The Forsaken One." Sermon, Duke Street Church, London, August 13, 2002.

_____. "The Lord Reigns." Scottish Reformed Conference, Hamilton College, South Lankarshire, Scotland, 2007.

_____. "The Scandal of Forgiveness." Sermon, Duke Street Church, London, October 16, 2005.

Helm, David. "Psalm 110." Sermon, Holy Trinity Church, Chicago, IL, January 4, 2009.

Horton, Michael. "Textual Narcissism." *White Horse Inn* podcast, November 27, 2010.

Jones, Andrew. "Sex and the City—Song of Songs." Sermon series, St. Helen's Bishopsgate Church, London, February, 2003.

Keller, Timothy J. "The Doctrine of Salvation." Sermon, Redeemer Presbyterian Church, New York, April 7, 2004.

_____. "Sexuality and the Christian Hope." Sermon, Redeemer Presbyterian Church, New York, April 18, 2004.

_____. "The Sinner." Sermon, Redeemer Presbyterian Church, New York, February 29, 2004.

Long, V. Phillips. Lecture notes from Psalms and Wisdom Literature. Covenant Theological Seminary, Summer 2006.

Ortlund, Raymond C. "The Love of God." Sermon, Christ Presbyterian Church, Nashville, TN, June 6, 2004.

_____. Untitled sermon on Ecclesiastes. Christ Presbyterian Church, Nashville, TN, July 17, 2005.

_____. "What the Bible Is All About." Sermon, Christ Presbyterian Church, Nashville, TN, June 19, 2005.

_____. "What Will Heaven Be Like?" Sermon, Christ Presbyterian Church, Nashville, TN, August 7, 2005.

Piper, John. "A Broken and Contrite Heart God Will Not Despise." Sermon, Bethlehem Baptist Church, Minneapolis, MN, June 8, 2008.

_____. "We Will All Stand before the Judgment of God." Sermon, Bethlehem Baptist Church, Minneapolis, MN, October 30, 2005.

_____. "Why the Gift of Prophecy Is Not the Usual Way of Knowing God's Will." Sermon, Bethlehem Baptist Church, Minneapolis, MN, April 1, 1990.

Woodhouse, John. "The Message of the Psalms." Sermon, Christ Church, St. Ives, Australia, April 22, 2001.

_____. "Psalm 1: The Secure Life." Sermon, Christ Church, St. Ives, Australia, April 29, 2001.

_____. "Psalm 2: The Lord and His Christ." Sermon, Christ Church, St. Ives, Australia, June 5, 2001.

_____. "The Psalms in the Bible." Proclamation Trust. http://www.proc trust.org.uk./product/instruction-on-series/instructions-on-psalms-david-and-christ-597.

_____. "The Psalms and Christ." Proclamation Trust. http://www.proc trust.org.uk./product/instruction-on-series/instructions-on-psalms-david-and-christ-597.

_____. "The Psalms and the Gospel." Proclamation Trust. http://www. proctrust.org.uk./product/instruction-on-series/instructions-on-psalms-david-and-christ-597.

_____. "Study Case—Guidance." Moore College, Sydney, Australia, undated.

Notes

Week 1: The Wisdom Hidden in the Wisdom Books

1. John Piper described his experience in this regard saying, in his message "How Important Is the Bible?" at Lausanne 2010, "God talks to me no other way, but don't get this wrong, he talks to me very personally. I open my Bible in the morning to meet my friend, my Savior, my Creator, my Sustainer. I meet him and he talks to me. . . . I'm not denying providence, not denying circumstances, not denying people; I'm just saying that the only authoritative communion I have with God with any certainty comes through the words of this book."

2. In Graeme Goldsworthy, *Gospel and Wisdom*, in *The Goldsworthy Trilogy: Gospel and Kingdom, Gospel and Wisdom, The Gospel in Revelation* (Exeter: Paternoster, 2000), 540. Goldsworthy writes, "If we are to understand the biblical view of guidance, we need to look at it in the context of the progressive nature of revelation. The truth of God's revelation comes by stages until it reaches the full intensity of the light of the knowledge of God in Christ. There are two things to be said about guidance in this biblical framework. First, guidance of individuals by direct means of dreams, visions and prophetic word decreases as the repository of God's revealed will grows. This does not mean that such direct and supernatural guidance necessarily ceases once the canon of Scripture is completed, but it does mean that the likelihood of God adding to his final word in Christ recorded in the New Testament is very remote indeed. I believe it is accurate to say that every case of special guidance given to individuals in the Bible has to do with that person's place in the outworking of God's saving purposes. To put it another way, there are no instances in the Bible in which God gives special and specific guidance to the ordinary believing Israelite or Christian in the details of their personal existence."

3. Ibid., 533.

4. Ibid., 499.

5. D. A. Carson, *The Cross and Christian Ministry: Leadership Lessons from 1 Corinthians* (Grand Rapids, MI: Baker, 2006), 23.

6. Adapted from "Why the Gift of Prophecy Is Not the Usual Way of Knowing God's Will," John Piper, Bethlehem Baptist Church, Minneapolis, MN, April 1, 1990.

7. Randy Alcorn, *Heaven* (Carol Stream, IL: Tyndale, 2004), 308.

8. Ibid., 396.

9. This beautiful picture of what God intends to show "in the coming ages" is adapted from Ray Ortlund Jr., "What Will Heaven Be Like?" sermon given at Christ Presbyterian Church, Nashville, TN, August 7, 2005.

Week 2: Job

1. Derek Kidner, *The Wisdom of Proverbs, Job, and Ecclesiastes* (Downers Grove, IL: Inter-Varsity, 1985), 61.

Week 3: Psalms: The Songs of Jesus

1. Adapted from Gordon D. Fee and Douglas K. Stuart, *How to Read the Bible for All Its Worth: a Guide to Understanding the Bible.* (Grand Rapids, MI: Zondervan, 1982), 189, which reads, "One needs to be aware that Hebrew poetry, by its very nature, was addressed, as it were, to the mind through the heart (i.e., much of the language is intentionally emotive). Therefore, one needs to be careful of over-exegeting the Psalms by finding special meanings in every word or phrase, where the poet may have intended none."

2. From 1974's Blue Swede version of "Hooked on a Feeling" written by Mark James in 1968.

3. From "Feelings," Loulou Gaste, lyrics; Morris Albert, recording, 1975.

4. In the printed version of his lectures for the class, *Psalms and Wisdom Literature* offered at Covenant Seminary in the summer of 2006, V. Philips Long quotes Derek Kidner as saying, "If in the law and prophets the dominant voice is God speaking to man, in the books we will be studying we find inspired examples of man's response to God (the Psalms) or to life (the wisdom books), which despite its perplexities is nonetheless seen as God's world over which He is sovereign." His original source for this quote is not given.

5. These final two sentences are adapted from the following statement in Tremper Longman, *How to Read the Psalms* (Downers Grove, IL: InterVarsity, 1988), 81. Longman writes, "In the Psalms, however, the negative always leads to the positive. Doubt leads to trust; anger toward God turns to love; sadness to joy."

6. See the first book in the Seeing Jesus in the Old Testament series, *The Promised One: Seeing Jesus in Genesis* (Wheaton, IL: Crossway, 2011).

7. Christopher Wright, *Knowing Jesus through the Old Testament* (Downers Grove, IL: InterVarsity, 1992), 108.

Week 4: Blessing and Perishing in the Psalms

1. Content in the previous three paragraphs relies heavily upon material adapted from *Psalms and Wisdom Notes: A Working Draft by Dr. Jay Sklar,* handouts for a class taught by Dr. Sklar at Covenant Theological Seminary, Fall 2009, 73–74.

2. Derek Kidner, *Psalms 1–72* (Downers Grove, IL: InterVarsity, 1973), 47.

3. I am indebted to John Woodhouse ("Psalm 1: The Secure Life," sermon, Christ Church, St. Ives, Australia, April 29, 2001), for the following approach to tracing "the man" throughout the Old Testament into the New.

4. The series of insights in this paragraph on Christ as the blessed man of Psalm 1 are drawn from the syllabus for "Preaching the Gospel in a Post-Modern World," taught by Timothy J. Keller at Reformed Theological Seminary, January 2002.

5. Ibid.

6. I was greatly helped in my understanding of "the books" and "the book of life" by John Piper, "We Will All Stand Before the Judgment of God," sermon, Bethlehem Baptist Church, October 30, 2005.

Week 5: The Royal Psalms

1. I was helped greatly in this section by Richard Belcher Jr., "The Royal Psalms," in *The Messiah and the Psalms* (Ross-shire, Scotland: Christian Focus, 2006).

2. For the following general outline of Psalm 2, I am indebted to Liam Goligher, "The Lord Reigns," sermon, 2007 Scottish Reformed Conference, Hamilton College, South Lankarshire, Scotland.

3. This linguistic background is provided by Mark Futato, *Transformed by Praise: The Purpose and Message of the Psalms* (Phillipsburg, NJ: P&R, 2002), 106.

4. Goligher, "The Lord Reigns."

Week 6: Repentance in the Psalms

1. John Piper, "A Broken and Contrite Heart God Will Not Despise," sermon, Bethlehem Baptist Church, Minneapolis, MN, June 8, 2008.

2. Tim Keller asked this penetrating application question in his sermon on Psalm 51, "The Sinner," Redeemer Presbyterian Church, New York, NY, February 29, 2004.

3. Ibid.

4. Because we read that David "sent messengers and took her," it would appear that this was not consensual. Bathsheba had no power to refuse the king.

5. This history on hyssop and its use in temple ceremonies comes from James Montgomery Boice, *Psalms*, vol. 2, Psalms 42–106 (Grand Rapids, MI: Baker, 1996), 429.

6. This understanding of what David meant when asking to be purged with hyssop is adapted from Liam Goligher, "The Scandal of Forgiveness," sermon, Duke Street Church, London, October 16, 2005.

7. Lewis E. Jones, "There Is Power in the Blood," 1899.

8. Tremper Longman III, *How to Read the Psalms* (Downers Grove, IL: InterVarsity, 1988), 57.

Week 7: The Suffering and Glory of Messiah in the Psalms

1. Christopher J. H. Wright, *Knowing Jesus through the Old Testament* (Downers Grove, IL: InterVarsity, 1992), *ix*.

2. This idea of David's expressing his own experience in stretched poetic language, going from literal description of his personal experience into hyperbole, is adapted from a statement by Sinclair Ferguson in his sermon "Divine Sufferer," Park Cities Presbyterian Church, Dallas, TX, November 17, 2004.

3. A. Bentzen, *King and Messiah* (Cambridge: Lutterworth Press, 1955), 94, n.40, quoted by Derek Kidner, *Psalms 1–72* (Downers Grove, IL: InterVarsity, 1973), 105.

4. Liam Goligher provides this literal translation of the Hebrew in "The Forsaken One," sermon, Duke Street Church in London, August 13, 2002.

5. Dick Lucas described this Old Testament custom in his sermon on Psalm 22, given in the "Studies in the Psalms" sermon series, St. Helen's Bishopsgate, London, February 15, 1976.

6. Sinclair Ferguson, "Divine Sufferer," sermon, Park Cities Presbyterian Church, Dallas, TX, November 17, 2004.

Week 8: Proverbs

1. This imagery of Proverbs 8:22–31 as a résumé for wisdom is adapted from Christopher Ash, "Jesus the Wisdom of God," sermon, All Saints, Little Shelford, England, February 21, 1999.

2. Derek Kidner writes: "To me it is clear that while some of this language was destined to prepare the way for the New Testament's Christology, the portrait in its own context is personifying a concept, not describing a personality" (*The Wisdom of Proverbs, Job and Ecclesiastes*, [Downers Grove, IL: InterVarsity, 1985], 23).

Week 9: Ecclesiastes

1. Graeme Goldsworthy, *The Goldsworthy Trilogy: Gospel and Kingdom, Gospel and Wisdom, The Gospel in Revelation* (Exeter: Paternoster, 2000), 499.

2. I am indebted to Kevin DeYoung's sermon "Welcome to College: It's Nothing but Vanity," University Reformed Church, Lansing, MI, August 24, 2008, for the general framework of reading Ecclesiastes as narrator using Qoheleth's words as a foil. DeYoung also states, "Most commentators see Qoheleth as all bad, which means you have to manipulate some texts. Others want to make him all good, and then you really have to rescue texts where he seems hopeless. Better is to be realistic; he is someone who gets some things right and some things wrong."

3. Ray Ortlund Jr., from his untitled sermon on Ecclesiastes, Christ Presbyterian Church, Nashville, Tennessee, July 17, 2005.

4. Bill Baldwin offers this alternate translation of the Hebrew in his unpublished notes on Ecclesiastes, http://bettercovenant.wordpress.com/2009/04/13/ecclesiastes/.

5. Ibid.

Week 10: Song of Solomon

1. Kathleen Buswell Nielson, *Ecclesiastes and Song of Songs: Wisdom's Searching and Finding* (Phillipsburg, NJ: P&R, 2009), 133.

2. Adapted from Nielson, who writes, "Seeing this structure at work in the Song of Songs allows us to read the poetry as an organic and coherent series of love songs, rather than a dramatic sequence to be fit into our own logical molds" (*Ecclesiastes and Song of Songs*, 134.

3. Except perhaps in Song 8:6, which refers to the "flame of the LORD." While God is not explicitly mentioned in Song of Solomon, he is assumed throughout.

4. Tom Gledhill, *The Message of the Song of Songs: The Lyrics of Love* (Leicester: Inter-Varsity, 1994), 39.

5. I gained great insight by listening to Andrew Jones's four-part sermon series *Sex and the City*, St. Helen's Bishopsgate Church, London. This idea comes specifically from the sermon "The Dark Side of Sex," delivered on February 11, 2003.

6. Duane A. Garrett, *Proverbs, Ecclesiastes, Song of Songs* (Nashville, TN: Broadman, 1993), 378.

7. Timothy Keller, "The Gospel and Sex," 2010, http://Redeemercitytocity.com.

8. Andrew Jones, "There's More to Life Than Sex," sermon, St. Helen's Bishopsgate Church, London, February 25, 2003.

9. Ibid.

10. This question is adapted from a similar question asked in Raymond C. Ortlund Jr., "The Love of God," sermon delivered at Christ Presbyterian Church, Nashville, TN, June 6, 2004.

11. Lyrics from the nineteenth-century hymn "Here Is Love," written by William Rees (1826–1899).

For additional content, downloads,
and resources for leaders, please visit:

www.SeeingJesusInTheOldTestament.com

Also Available in the *Seeing Jesus in the Old Testament* Series

The Wisdom of God DVD

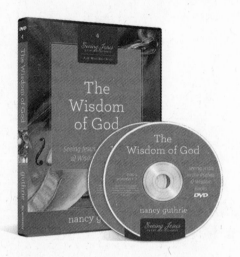

Go deeper in your study of the Psalms and Wisdom Books with the 10-episode DVD companion to the Bible Study, *The Wisdom of God*.

The Wisdom of God DVD // 978-1-4335-3451-5

The Promised One: Seeing Jesus in Genesis Book and DVD

The Promised One provides a fresh look at the book of Genesis, leading readers in discovering how its stories, symbols, people, and promises point to Christ. A ten-session DVD companion is also available.

The Promised One // 978-1-4335-2625-1
The Promised One DVD // 978-1-4335-3221-4

SeeingJesusInTheOldTestament.com

Also Available in the *Seeing Jesus in the Old Testament* Series

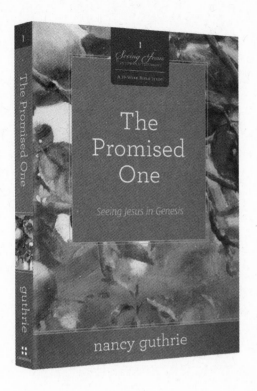

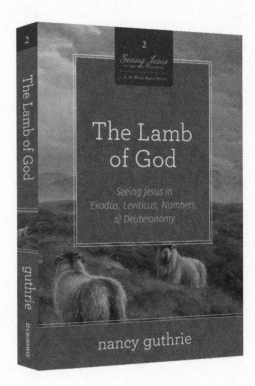

A ten-session DVD companion is also available for each study.

Coming in June 2013!

The Son of David
Seeing Jesus in the Historical Books

SeeingJesusInTheOldTestament.com